HEART & SOUL

The Kurt Warner Story

Text by Gary Ronberg
Photos by Marc Serota

TRIUMPH
BOOKS

This book is available in quantity at special discounts for your group or organization. For further information, contact:

Triumph Books
542 South Dearborn Street
Suite 750
Chicago, Illinois 60605
(312) 939-3330
Fax (312) 663-3557
www.triumphbooks.com

Printed in U.S.A.

ISBN: 978-1-60078-310-4

Design by Barry Stock

All photos courtesy of Marc Serota except P. 2, 3, 12–13, and 122 courtesy of Marc Wallheiser; P. i, 39, and 44–45 courtesy of Getty Images; and P. 36–37, 46, 48–49, 88, 92–93, 96, 98, 99, and 100–101 courtesy of AP Images.

Table Of Contents

Despite great playing from Warner, the
Cardinals simply could not defeat the
Steelers in Super Bowl XLIII.

SUPER BOWL
XLIII

In January 2005 the Arizona Cardinals called a news conference at their corporate headquarters in Tempe.

The old bird was gone.

Often derided as a parakeet anyway (especially during gluts of losing), the cardinal that had been the team's logo since its move from Chicago to St. Louis in 1960 had been retooled. In its place was an angry cardinal etched in black, with an evil eye, gold beak, and nasty feathers.

"A tough bird," team owner Bill Bidwill said. "Hopefully, it will be worn by tougher and faster and meaner players."

A predator. "It's not the size of the bird in the fight," coach Dennis Green said. "It's the size of the fight in the bird."

Among the Cardinals players at the news conference was Josh McCown, a quarterback who had been raised in the hills of East Texas. Asked if he knew anything about tough birds, McCown said, "The only birds I know about are the ones you shoot. Like a duck or a dove or quail.

"You're not really supposed to shoot a cardinal, and I don't know if I'd shoot this one. It looks so mean, it might pull out a gun and shoot back."

Warner walks off the field after losing to the Steelers in Super Bowl XLIII.

By Sunday, February 1, 2009, in Tampa, Florida, the nation's economy had inflicted a few dents in the annual profligacy of Super Bowl week. Even so, private jets still had been landing, limos cruising, cocktail glasses clinking, and media hyping. Tickets had been sold for thousands of dollars, and TV ads had been sold for millions. And now, as the activities preceding Super Bowl XLIII were beamed around the world, Raymond James Stadium was rife with Pittsburgh Steelers black and yellow and white Terrible Towels swirling from its highest reaches to the emerald grass below. The scarce swatches of red and white merely underscored the startling presence of the Arizona Cardinals, a franchise that had not appeared in even a National Football League Championship Game in 61 years.

> "There was plenty of opportunity to wonder if I would ever start again," Warner said. "Would I ever be back here? Would I ever get another chance to start?"

Their quarterback, Kurt Warner, had been here before. Twice his last-minute heroics had elevated games to the ranks of the best ever played—in 2000 during the St. Louis Rams' 23–17 victory over the Tennessee Titans and two years later in the Rams' haunting 20–17 loss to the New England Patriots. What made Warner's encore so astonishing on this night was that only three years earlier he had been released by the Rams and New York Giants, too dinged and declining.

"There was plenty of opportunity to wonder if I would ever start again," Warner said. "Would I ever be back here? Would I ever get another chance to start?"

In 2005 joining the lowly Cardinals did not appear to be the best of career moves. But few NFL teams were interested in him at all, and none wanted him as a starter. Warner recalled, "I think the perception [of Kurt Warner] was that he couldn't play anymore anyway, there was no more football left in him, and he was basically trying to survive. So he goes to Arizona, an organization that hasn't won, they bring in a guy because of his name, and it's going to be the same as always. The Cardinals don't win, and Kurt Warner can't play."

For whatever reason, Warner sensed that the Cardinals had suddenly gotten serious about winning. Was it the new $455 million stadium going up in Glendale or per-haps the drafting of such gifted receivers as Anquan Boldin in 2003 and Larry Fitzgerald in 2004? One Arizona blogger offered up the Cardinals' new logo as the reason. "Of the 15 current NFL teams symbolized by animals," he wrote, "birds surprisingly outnumber cats by 5 to 4. Of this group, the cardinal is the only non-predatory bird, subsisting on seeds, nuts, and berries. I don't think it's too much of a stretch to say that the white part of the eye now references carnivorousness."

As it turned out, an initial case of risk-reward for both parties yielded glory

> "I think the perception [of Kurt Warner] was that he couldn't play anymore anyway, there was no more football left in him, and he was basically trying to survive."

Warner hands off during the Cardinals' loss to the Steelers in Super Bowl XLIII.

Casey Hampton tries to stop Warner as he throws one of his many memorable passes during Super Bowl XLIII on February 1, 2009.

Warner lofts a pass high and long over the head of the Steelers' James Harrison.

neither could have envisioned. "I think the Cardinals knew something a lot of people didn't or took a chance on something a lot of people wouldn't," Warner said. "I knew I could still play, given the right opportunity. So the Cardinals took a chance, I took a chance, and together we made something special happen."

By the opening game of the 2008 season, Warner, at 37, was a starting quarterback in the NFL again. The Cardinals won their first two games, lost twice, then flew to 7–3 and the NFC West title before struggling to finish 9–7 in the regular season. It was in the playoffs that Warner caught fire. In victories over Atlanta and Carolina, he completed 40 of 64 passes for 491 yards, four touchdowns, and two interceptions. Against Philadelphia for the NFC title, he connected on 21 of 28 attempts for 279 yards, four touchdowns, and no interceptions. Included in his glowing 145.7 rating against the Eagles was the spellbinding 14-play, 72-yard drive and winning touchdown pass in the final minutes of the 32–25 triumph that put Arizona in Super Bowl XLIII against the Pittsburgh Steelers.

The Steelers and old Chicago Cardinals were among the NFL's charter members in 1933 (during World War II they even combined rosters for a team they called "PittCard" in 1944). But since the dawn of the Super Bowl era in 1966, the franchises had gone in opposite directions. Up went the Steelers to tie Dallas and San Francisco with five NFL world championships each. Down went the Cardinals, not only in the standings but also on the Mississippi River to St. Louis in 1960. And 28 years later they were on the move again, this time to the desert of the Southwest.

Warner looks for an open receiver as he drops back to pass in Super Bowl XLIII.

Coming into the 2009 Super Bowl, the Steelers were seeking their second world championship in four years and a record sixth in NFL history. The Cardinals had not won so much as a playoff game since 1948.

Their matchup was most intriguing, however, as it presented the classic clash of a great offense against a great defense. Primarily because of a defense reminiscent of its vaunted Steel Curtain in the 1970s, the Steelers arrived in Tampa with an 11–4 record in the regular season and triumphs over San Diego and Baltimore in NFC East title games. In fact, Pittsburgh's Dick LeBeau—for more than 30 years an architect of splendid NFL defenses and author of the fabled "zone blitz"—suggested that "sideline to sideline" this year's Steelers defense was the best he'd ever coached.

His All-Pro safety, Troy Polamalu, was inclined to agree. "Without a doubt, this is the best defense I've ever played on," he said. "This team had to rely more on defense. We had to make a lot more big plays. We caused and forced a lot more turnovers than in the past."

With NFL Defensive Player of the Year James Harrison and LaMarr Woodley charging from the outside, the Steelers were certain to exert enormous pressure on Warner. Pittsburgh hadn't allowed an opponent to throw for 300 yards all year. Still, they hadn't faced a quarterback so adroit as Warner at shredding blitz patterns.

A man of few words, James Harrison said, "They have two good running backs and three receivers with over 1,000 yards."

Of Warner, Polamalu said, "He's pretty much seen all the defenses this game has to offer. From a schematic standpoint, you just try to give him different looks."

"He knows what to expect and doesn't let anything rattle him," said Steelers defensive end Brett Keisel. "We're hoping to change that."

In addition to stalking Warner, the Steelers also had to shackle the Cardinals' elegant All-Pro wide receiver, Larry Fitzgerald. A one-man highlight reel, Fitzgerald arrived in Tampa with 23 receptions for 419 yards and five touchdowns in the postseason alone.

"Larry Fitzgerald is quite simply the best receiver in the world down the field in one-on-one situations," said Pittsburgh head coach Mike Tomlin. "We need to limit the number of times we're downfield with him one-on-one. Invariably, he's going to come up with the football. The tape tells us that."

On the defensive side of the football, the Cardinals were not to be underestimated. Rising to the drama of postseason play, in three games they had sacked the quarterback seven times, intercepted eight passes, and yielded an average of 77 yards per game rushing. Only twice had they given up touchdowns on the ground.

The key to the Steelers' attack was 6'5", 240-pound Ben Roethlisberger. At 26 Roethlisberger was a fine young quarterback, to be sure, but he had struggled at times during the regular season. He was also still overshadowed by his performance in Pittsburgh's 21–10 victory over Seattle in the 2004 Super Bowl, when he completed just nine of 21 passes for just 123 yards, no touchdowns, and two interceptions. His 22.6 passer rating in that Super Bowl was still the lowest for the quarterback of a winning team.

"I played really bad, and that kind of eats at you," Roethlisberger said. "I do want to play better than I did. The first time, my play didn't help the team win. It almost helped us lose. This time I'm not going to say it's all on my shoulders. But if I turn the ball over and play poorly, it's not going to help our offense, and it's not going to win this game."

He admitted that he never really got control of his first appearance on the big stage. "That was the first time I stayed nervous for an entire game," he said. "I expect it to be different this time. I've been here before and kind of understand what went right and what went wrong last time. You have to get over the initial hoopla, the flash, the lights. Don't get too overwhelmed with it."

> "I think about that game more than any I've ever played in," Warner said. "That year we were favored, we were expected to win, and when you don't win you feel like you missed an opportunity to make history. It's something that sticks with you, and it'll probably stick with me for a lifetime."

Warner could relate to that, though not so much with nerves as with the seven years he had lived with the residue of some mistakes he'd made in his second Super Bowl. In 2002 the Rams had arrived at the New Orleans Superdome favored by 14 points over the New England Patriots. Warner went on to complete 28 of 44 passes for 365 yards and a touchdown, but he also was intercepted twice—once by Ty Law for 47 yards and a touchdown in the Patriots' 20–17 upset.

"I think about that game more than any I've ever played in," Warner said. "That year we were favored, we were expected to win, and when you don't win you feel like you missed an opportunity to make history. It's something that sticks

with you, and it'll probably stick with me for a lifetime."

True to form, Warner was pragmatic about the challenges posed by a Pittsburgh defensive unit highlighted by the daunting presence of Harrison. "They're going to throw things at us we've never seen before," he said. "Our recognition of what they're doing and where they're coming from, who we're blocking and who are the free guys— that's going to be a huge key."

Though they won the coin toss, the Cardinals elected to kick off to the Steelers. Was second-year head coach Ken Whisenhunt, who had been Pittsburgh's offensive co-ordinator from 2001 to 2006, putting Roethlisberger's nerves to the test?

The Steelers quickly and smartly marched 61 yards to the Arizona 1-yard line. On third-and-goal, Roethlisberger appeared to bull his way for a touchdown. On the Cardinals sideline, Whisenhunt dropped his red flag in protest. After being reviewed by NFL officials, the play was reversed. The Steelers settled for an 18-yard field goal by Jeff Reed.

On their next possession, the Steelers drove 70 yards in eight plays for a 10–0 advantage. Their touchdown came on Gary Russell's one-yard run. Roethlisberger was sharp and confident, a field general personified. In fact, it was the Cardinals who appeared somewhat awestruck by where they were.

Warner in action in Super Bowl XLIII.

Cardinals team photo
before Super Bowl XLIII.

Warner took care of that. Completing seven of nine passes for 92 yards, including a 45-yarder to Boldin, he promptly swept the Cardinals 83 yards in nine plays and a one-yard touchdown pass to tight end Ben Patrick. With 8:34 remaining in the half, Pittsburgh's lead had been sliced to 10–7.

Moments later came the play that may well be remembered as the most shocking of all that had been run since Super Bowl I in 1966. The scene was set two minutes before halftime, when Cardinals linebacker Karlos Dansby snatched a tipped Roethlisberger pass out of the air at the Pittsburgh 34-yard line. Smelling Steelers blood, Warner whipped passes of 10 yards to Robert Hightower, 12 yards to Fitzgerald, and seven and four yards to Boldin for a first down at the 1-yard line. There he called timeout with :18 remaining.

After a sideline discussion with offensive coordinator Todd Haley and Whisenhunt, Warner split Boldin outside Fitzgerald in the left slot. The play stipulated that as Fitzgerald broke left on a corner route to the outside, Boldin would cut beneath him on a right slant into the end zone. Excellent call.

Or so it appeared until Pittsburgh's James Harrison, after crowding the line as if to blitz, suddenly dropped back and to his right—directly in the path of Warner's pass to Boldin.

"I don't think Warner ever saw James," said Pittsburgh's LeBeau, the zone-blitz author.

"They showed an all-out blitz," Warner said. "James did an excellent job holding in at the line, then popping out. I couldn't see him through our linemen. I thought I had Anquan for a second, but James jumped out there and made the play."

"It was kind of like, 'Just give it time,'" said Harrison. "I slid over to the right, he threw it into my hands, and I took off."

Cradling his purloined pigskin in his right arm, Harrison bolted to the right and launched himself on a Clydesdale lope that would carry him 100 yards into the Arizona end zone and instant Super Bowl immortality. On their sideline, the Steelers erupted. "All we kept thinking was, You've got to score! You've got to score! Time's running out!" Roethlisberger recalled.

As the 6'5", 240-pound Harrison lumbered along the Arizona sideline, his journey appeared to unfold in slow motion as he shrugged off Warner's desperate dive, lurched past a tumbling Tim Hightower, then plowed through the speeding Fitzgerald and Steve Breaston as they closed in from behind.

The referee's arms shot up in the night lights. Exhausted, Harrison lay sprawled on his back, arms outstretched, chest and torso heaving. "Those last couple yards were tougher than anything I've ever done in my life," he said.

At halftime, as they yielded the stadium floor to Bruce Springsteen, the Cardinals were stunned at what could—should?—have been. Instead of leading this, the game of their lives, by 14–10—or at least tied at 10—they would begin its third quarter trailing the five-time champions 17–7. "If only we could have brought him down," Warner would say.

Still dazed, perhaps, in the third quarter, the Cardinals committed three personal fouls on an 11-play drive that consumed almost nine minutes and presented the Steelers with a 20–7 lead after Reed's 21-yard field goal. There were several damning infractions, including a face-mask call against rookie corner Dominique Rodgers-Cromartie with Pittsburgh second-and-13 from its own 15. Moments later, Dansby was flagged for roughing the quarterback.

Yet again, just as after the Cardinals had fallen behind in the first quarter by 10, Warner seized the initiative. Starting from their 13 with 11:40 to play, he orchestrated an 86-yard drive with seven straight completions to the Pittsburgh 1.

All night the Steelers had doubled up on Fitzgerald, bracing him at the line of scrimmage and rerouting him whenever possible. To this, Warner responded with telling throws to Boldin, Breaston, and running back Edgerrin James out of the backfield. But now, with this monumental march and a yard to go in the end zone, it was time for Fitzgerald—to whom Warner had thrown only once.

Warner feathered a lovely pass to Fitzgerald just inches beyond Steelers cornerback Ike Taylor. Fitzgerald made a sensational one-handed catch while tumbling to the grass, and with the touchdown and extra point, the Cardinals trailed 20–14.

Following an exchange of punts, the Steelers found themselves first-and-10 from their 1-yard line. After two plays,

> Moments later came the play that may well be remembered as the most shocking of all that had been run since Super Bowl I in 1966. The scene was set two minutes before halftime, when Cardinals linebacker Karlos Dansby snatched a tipped Roethlisberger pass out of the air at the Pittsburgh 34-yard line. Smelling Steelers blood, Warner whipped passes of 10 yards to Robert Hightower, 12 yards to Fitzgerald, and seven and four yards to Boldin for a first down at the 1-yard line.

Roethlisberger retreated into his end zone again. There, a holding penalty generated an automatic safety. Pittsburgh's lead had been trimmed to four points.

The Steelers punted away from their 20, and the Cardinals took possession at their 36.

And two plays later, it was Fitzgerald's turn again. As Warner took the snap in shotgun formation, Fitzgerald, wide right, sped 15 yards upfield before darting left, leaving Taylor in his wake. When Polamalu was an instant tardy to cover, a meadow of green appeared at midfield. Taking Warner's perfect spiral in stride, Fitzgerald set sail for the end zone— so free that he watched himself running on the giant screen above his destination!

With the extra point, the score became 23–20, Cardinals, with only 2:37 remaining to play. Polamalu said, "It was like a shot in the heart."

Never in 42 Super Bowls had a team rallied from 13 points down in the fourth quarter. Was this now the greatest comeback victory ever? Pittsburgh coach Mike Tomlin said, "If they score, that's how you want them to do it. You don't want them to milk the clock."

After the kickoff, with the ball at their 22-yard line, Roethlisberger addressed his teammates. No jangled nerves now. Never before in this game, and not now. He said, "It's now or never, guys. You'll be remembered forever if you do this. All the film study, all the hard work, all the stuff about us, it will be for nothing if we don't do this. We have to go out and do it."

In the huddle, wide receiver Santonio Holmes piped up: "Ben, I want the ball in my hands no matter what, no matter where it is."

On the first play, this was the call: "Holding, offense! Ten-yard penalty. First down."

From their 12-yard line, the Steelers made four yards in two plays. On third-and-6 from the 26, Roethlisberger again scrambled for time before rifling the ball 14 yards to Holmes. Often criticized during the regular season for taking too many sacks and having too many fumbles, on this night Roethlisberger had been the bellwether, clambering about, shedding and eluding tacklers, buying time until a receiver—now Holmes!—broke free.

On the Cardinals sideline, all Kurt Warner could do was watch.

Roethlisberger threw to Holmes again, this time for 13. Then there was a scramble for four. A field-goal attempt loomed. Three points to tie for sudden death. First overtime Super Bowl ever. (In the wake of this drama, why not?)

Another short and safe pass to Holmes. Suddenly he was clear, weaving his way 40 yards to the Arizona 6. He'd said he wanted that ball.

First down, 48 seconds to go. To Holmes again, in the left corner. Through his fingers. No matter.

On second down, Roethlisberger retreated to pass. He searched the end zone— "Scramble left, scramble right, find somebody open!" he would say—once, twice, three times he pumped the ball. And then he threw the prettiest pass you will ever see, just beyond the outstretched arms of Cardinals cornerback Ralph Brown, just before Cardinals safety Aaron Francisco got there, into the reaching gloved fingers of Santonio "Toner" Holmes, big toes on the grass inside the stripe, ball against the 10 on his chest, falling face mask first to glory. "I knew it was good," Holmes would say. "All I did was stand up on my toes and extend my hands."

The clock glowed 00:35.

Moments later, it was over.

The following night, after flying up to New York, Ben Roethlisberger described the decisive play on *The Late Show with David Letterman*.

"I was getting ready to start running," he said, "and when I saw about five guys closing in on me, I knew my life was about to end. I saw Santonio in the corner, and as soon as I let it go, I saw the defensive back going to get it, and I thought the game was over. I blew it. He made a heck of a catch."

With catches for 131 yards, including all but five of the 78 on the final march, Holmes

> Yet again, just as after the Cardinals had fallen behind in the first quarter by 10, Warner seized the initiative. Starting from their 13 with 11:40 to play, he orchestrated an 86-yard drive with seven straight completions to the Pittsburgh 1.

would be the Most Valuable Player of a Super Bowl game with the most candidates ever.

Thirty-five seconds later, after Warner had been stripped of the ball and hauled down at midfield, it was over.

"You can't explain it," said Polamalu. "You are seconds away from crying in your locker room and them being out there. That's how amazing this is."

The Cardinals were in shock. "It was like getting a chair pulled out from under you," Fitzgerald said.

In light of what they had accomplished in a single incomparable season, however— their first playoff victory since 1948 and competing for their first NFL title since 1947—there was so much to savor.

"You've got to tip your hats to those guys," Warner said of the six-time-champion Steelers. "They fought to the end and made the plays when they counted."

He had just become the first quarterback ever to pass for 300 yards in three Super Bowls, completing 31 of 43 attempts for 377 yards and three touchdowns.

"I'm sitting here thinking about how great a season this was, how nobody expected us to be here, how nobody expected me to be here. We played a team nobody expected us to beat and had a chance to beat them in the last two minutes. We took the best team in the league down to the wire. Win or lose, I'm proud of this team. I think that's one of the reasons this doesn't hurt as bad as it could. I want to enjoy this great game we just played in."

The greatest of them all? Evidence swiftly accumulated that it was so.

"It was a game that left us all a bit breathless and kept reinventing itself in the midst of an unforgettable fourth quarter of lead changes and heroic plays," *Sports Illustrated* observed. "It was Harrison's night for the longest time, then Kurt Warner and the long-dormant Larry Fitzgerald stormed back to steal the spotlight but not the game. Because the game, and the Super Bowl championship, in the end was decided by the remarkable Ben Roethlisberger–to-Holmes connection in the extreme back right corner of the Steelers end zone. This was a game that, for three quarters, seemed like it would be defined by Harrison's one-of-a-kind touchdown, but the final 15 minutes rewrote the script again, and again, and again. Warner and Fitzgerald made magic, but the Steelers answered. Super Bowl XLIII was a fight to the end all right. A historic and entertaining fight that had more drama than we ever expected and have ever witnessed before."

To place the game in perspective for himself, Warner simply remembered 1999. That was the season a decade ago—only four years after he'd been stocking shelves at the Hy-Vee supermarket in Cedar Falls, Iowa—that he came off the bench and led the woeful St. Louis Rams to the greatest single-season turnabout in NFL history and victory in the Super Bowl.

"This game, and in '99 with the Rams when we were in similar situations—those things are what I'm going to take away more than anything when I leave this game," Kurt Warner said. "It's not going to be about touchdown passes thrown or games won. It's being part of two organizations that nobody expected anything from and making a run to the Super Bowl and exceeding expectations and changing perceptions of those two teams. My ultimate dream is that when I walk away, everybody who played with me or was in the organization I was with, says, 'We were a better team, we were a better organization, I'm a better player because I was around that guy.'

"That's what I want my legacy to be."

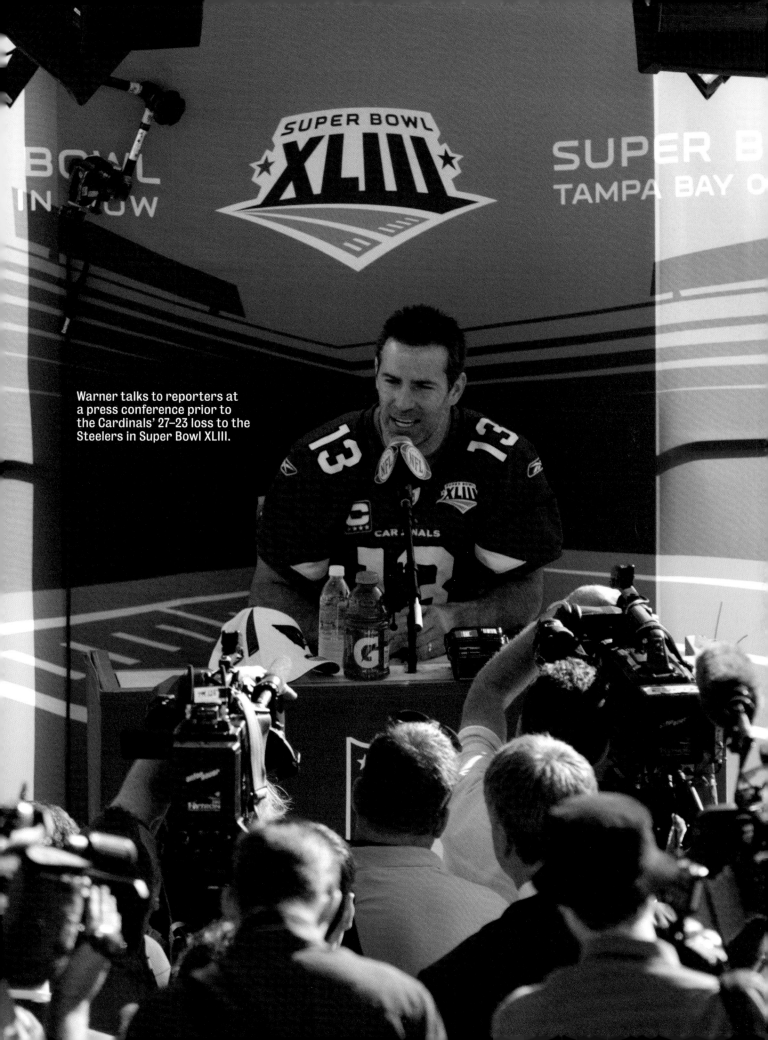

Warner talks to reporters at a press conference prior to the Cardinals' 27–23 loss to the Steelers in Super Bowl XLIII.

At Regis High School, Kurt was All-State in basketball and football.

· 2 ·
BIRTH OF A LEGEND

He grew up in Iowa, where the first settlers were Eastern Europeans who raised oats, corn, and wheat in what would become the breadbasket of America. Soon followed the English and the Irish, the Scots and the Scandinavians, who put down roots of their own and shared the dawn of their new lives with those who had come before.

As they evolved into fiercely proud Americans, all imbued the heartland with traits of the Old Country: hard work, respect, traditions, and church bells on Sunday. They waved at each other through their windshields and from the swings and chairs on their front porches. "People in Iowa are terrific," Kurt Warner says. "Some places you can be walking down the street, say hello to someone, they don't answer you. In Iowa you can start a conversation by saying hello."

Kurt and his older brother Matt.

In 1975, when he was four years old in Cedar Rapids, Iowa, his mother, Sue, a homemaker, and his father, Gene, a telephone linesman, divorced. Kurt and his older brother Matt spent weekdays with their mom and every other weekend with their dad. Their mom got a job at a company that manufactured plastic bags, and their dad arranged weekends around the things fathers and sons do together. When Gene remarried, he brought another Matt, the son of his new wife, Mimi, into the lives of his other two children. Before long all three were tight. "Never any stepbrother stuff," says Mimi's Matt. "We were brothers from the start. Always will be."

The boys' world revolved around sports, a good thing because sports kept a fractured family from falling apart altogether. Across the street was a cemetery where the boys and their friends played football and baseball. Next to it was a big backyard whose owners said it was okay to take a lawn mower and carve out the yard lines, sidelines, and end zones of a make-believe gridiron. From every Friday after school to Sundays at sundown, the boys were on that field. On autumn Saturdays they were the Iowa Hawkeyes in a Big Ten Conference; on Sundays they were the Dallas Cowboys or Green Bay Packers of the National Football League.

Mimi's Matt recalls, "In the back of one of our end zones was a vegetable garden. If we had a difference of opinion, some tomatoes flew."

The Warner boys grew up faster than most, particularly after their mother divorced a second time. They lived from week to week on her paycheck and the money her sons made in a store or around the neighborhood. They were good boys; getting into trouble was not an option.

At Regis High, a Catholic school of about 400 students, Kurt was All-State in basketball and football. "He had a unique confidence in himself," says Gene Warner. "He wasn't afraid of responsibility and pressure."

In the fall of his senior year Kurt received a letter from Hayden Fry, the head football coach at the University of Iowa, inviting him to a home game as a guest of the athletic department. Elated, Kurt and his mother drove to Iowa City, got a tour of 70,000-seat Kinnick Stadium, and met a few Hawkeyes players on the field. Iowa beat Northwestern that Saturday, but after the game Fry didn't even speak to Kurt and his mother. "It hurt," Warner recalls. "It hurt bad. I was probably the best quarterback in the state, and he never even shook my hand."

Iowa State, the state's only other major college, didn't come calling either. The lone offer was a partial scholarship to Division I-AAA Northern Iowa in Cedar Falls, where Warner was promised that after being redshirted his first year, he would compete for starting quarterback the next. Once on campus, however, Warner found himself behind a quarterback who would start—unchallenged—three seasons in row.

Warner thought about quitting football to play basketball. The coaches would hear nothing of it. He considered transferring somewhere else. His parents told him to stay where he was and get his degree.

> The Warner boys grew up faster than most, particularly after their mother divorced a second time. They lived from week to week on her paycheck and the money her sons made in a store or around the neighborhood. They were good boys; getting into trouble was not an option.

"You're building character," Sue Warner told her son.

"Mother," he replied. "I've got enough character. I don't need any more."

In his senior year, Warner lit up the Gateway Conference like he knew he could have all along. He led the conference in yards passing and total offense. Four times he threw for more than 300 yards in a game. Twice he was named Player of the Week. After Northern Iowa won the conference championship, Warner was named Gateway's Offensive Player of the Year.

On several occasions during the winter, Warner bumped into Fry at sports banquets, where the coach seemed to enjoy telling audiences how he'd overlooked this fine young quarterback.

In the weeks leading up to the college draft, Fry invited Warner to work out for NFL scouts at Kinnick Stadium. But when draft weekend arrived, Warner spent two days watching on TV—waiting for a phone call that never came.

"Rejection had become a pattern," Gene Warner recalls. "The beauty of it is, Kurt never gave up on himself."

The Packers and San Diego Chargers each offered him $5,000 to attend their

Two weeks after high school, Brenda headed to boot camp for the U.S. Marine Corps.

mini-camp. Warner chose Green Bay and flew to Arizona, where a limousine driver met his plane, carried his bags, and drove him to a very nice hotel. It went downhill from there. At one point, overwhelmed by complexities of the Green Bay offense, he even declined a coach's request to run a play.

Three months later, Warner was in the best form of his young life when the Packers opened training camp at St. Norbert's College in Wisconsin. He knew every play in the book; his throws were crisp and accurate. During the next six weeks, however, he ran only 12 plays in camp and didn't appear in one preseason game. When the phone rang in his dorm one morning, his instructions were brief: "Come downstairs. Bring your playbook."

Of the other three quarterbacks in camp, only Brett Favre, a future Hall of Famer, survived. Mark Brunell, a future All-Pro, and Ty Detmer, a Heisman Trophy winner, were traded. "All four did well," said quarterbacks coach Steve Mariucci. "It just took a little longer for Kurt to show what he could do."

Years later Mariucci would tell Warner that St. Norbert's College in August 1994 was neither the time nor the place for the

Kurt and Brenda take pleasure in reading the bible together. Christianity is the foundation of both of their lives.

quarterback from Northern Iowa. Green Bay had three quarterbacks. All had pro experience. Each made a lot of money. None would watch from the sideline as a rookie tried to prove himself on the field. "Mooch was right," Warner says. "I needed my experiences of the next five years to perform the way I can now."

At 17 Brenda Carney was an All-American cheerleader in high school. She was a senior in search of direction, excitement, a sense of accomplishment, and—most of all—a wondrous adventure!

Two weeks after she graduated from high school, she headed for Parris Island, South Carolina, and boot camp with the

United States Marine Corps. Brenda was so young that her parents' signatures were required for her to enlist.

The Marines were everything she had imagined and more. To this day she reveres every challenge the corps threw at her, its unearthing of strengths she might never have known she had. "I was able to send money back to my parents," Brenda says. "I still miss the camaraderie, the knowledge that every day everybody was ready to go.

"I hear people who skip an appointment say, 'I didn't feel like going.' I say to myself, 'How can you not go?'"

As a marine corporal, Brenda was assigned to Virginia and specialized in intelligence outside Washington, D.C. She had married a marine and given birth to their son, Zachary, four months earlier. One day her phone rang at work. It was her husband. He told her that their baby had stopped breathing in the bathtub.

They rushed their infant to the emergency room, where a battery of elaborate tests failed to reveal why the boy's brain continued to swell. The next day her hus-

Warner interacted wonderfully with Brenda's son Zach from the very beginning. Here the two ride four-wheelers in the snow.

Kurt and Brenda both value the virtues of family and togetherness.

band told Brenda what had happened. He had accidentally dropped their son in the bathtub, bumping the back of his head.

The doctors told them it was unlikely their son would survive. And even if he did, he would be blind, with little chance at a normal life. Brenda's prayers got her through the days and weeks in the hospital, through Zachary's violent seizures and illnesses, through the fears and anger she harbored. Zachary did survive. But with

no significant improvement, the doctors finally suggested their baby be taken home.

Brenda took an honorable discharge from the marine corps, and a year later her marriage began to unravel. She took Zach, moved back to Cedar Falls to live with her parents, and filed for divorce a month before giving birth to a baby daughter, Jesse Jo.

Her parents' home had two bedrooms, and after she arrived with her babies it be-

27

Warner's stellar career with the Rams brings a smile to his face.

came cramped and chaotic. When her boyfriend moved in two years later, the four of them moved downstairs to the basement.

They had met at Wild E. Coyote's, a country-and-western club near the Northern Iowa campus. Kurt was in his third season as the backup quarterback on the football team, and a teammate had taken him to the bar to cheer him up. Brenda had been to the place a few times with friends and even taken some line-dancing lessons there. Her mother had said she needed to get out of the house more often, that she and Brenda's dad would take care of the children.

Kurt and Brenda had noticed each other at the bar before.

"I saw this lady on the dance floor constantly," Kurt Warner recalls, "dancing with every guy in the place."

"I thought if someone got up the nerve to ask me to dance, I would," Brenda Warner says. "I do remember this good-looking guy who always had a bunch of people around him. Female, usually."

After their first night on the dance floor, Kurt walked Brenda to the parking lot, and she told him, "I've got two small children, I'm divorced, and [I] live with my parents. If I never hear from you again, I'll understand."

At 9:00 the next morning the doorbell rang, and he was on the doorstep, a single rose in hand.

"I was real protective of my kids," she says. "I would not let any guys meet my kids."

He smiled and said, "I want to meet the kids."

"For whatever reason, something inside me said to let him meet them," she says. "I really pray about what I consider the

Brenda's son Zach. Brenda was ver
protective of Zach in the early stage
of her and Kurt's relationsh

Spirit talking to me, and in Kurtis' case, I just felt like, 'Go with it.' So he's on the floor wrestling with Zachary, and I didn't even have time to explain that my son has brain damage and he's blind."

Warner liked her. He liked her a lot. She was smart, structured, her own person. "I found her very interesting, and she was a little bit older," he says. "Maybe I'd matured more in growing up and needed someone like that."

She sensed this. "I broke up with a guy to go out with Kurtis," she says. "The man I broke up with was a special-needs teacher from a strong family and a Catholic back-ground. He lived in Cedar Falls.

"Into my life comes this 21-year-old football player. Who knew what was going to happen? If I'd been looking for a father for my chil-dren, I wouldn't have picked him at all. He was just different. Better than anyone I'd ever dreamed of. I thought my life would be better if I stayed with him just because of the kind of person he is."

They had no money, and their dates amounted to playing with Zach and Jesse Jo. "He would come over," she says. "We'd order Domino's Pizza for $9 and wrestle on the floor with the kids and maybe watch a movie. Then he'd go home. That was our date. I mean, real cheap."

When Warner moved into their home, he was welcomed by Brenda's parents. Even so, he was embarrassed to be living there. He had a college degree. People liked him. But his obsessive pursuit of a pro football career had left him with no job and no apparent future. Family and friends couldn't figure out his relationship with Brenda, but they were intrigued by his sudden transition from BMOC to family man.

During the day Warner kept the embers of his NFL dreams aglow with two-hour

practices at his alma mater. The rest of the time he cared for Zach and Jesse Jo and babysat when Brenda attended classes at

32

Kurt and Brenda have come a long way since they lived in her parents' basement.

Hawkeye Community College.

"We were living on Brenda's food stamps and the aid she was getting for college," he says. "It was not the way I wanted to take care of her and the children."

-3-
THE IMPORTANCE
OF FAITH

Kurt at a Barnstormers
press conference.

"There were times I remember praying that no matter what I had to do, just praying that the lord would give me a job so that I could take care of my family. I didn't care if I had to work till I was 90."

—Kurt Warner

His prayers were answered. The night shift at the Hy-Vee supermarket in Cedar Falls was good, honest work. Among his duties were stocking shelves; cleaning up messes from broken jars; sweeping, mopping, and buffing the floors; bagging groceries; and walking customers to their cars and placing their purchases in the trunk. It was humbling, to be sure—a former star quarterback at the local university, rejected by the pros, now wearing a blue shirt with a name tag that read, "HELLO! MY NAME IS KURT."

Nobody ever asked what it was like for him, working at the Hy-Vee (after all, this was Iowa), but there were moments when he did wonder what people might be saying about him over their backyard fences. "I had surrendered whatever pride I had left," he says. "But I was making $5.50 an hour and darned happy to be getting it."

In the wee hours it wasn't unusual for a roll or two of toilet paper to arc the length of an aisle and settle into the bread-basket of a "receiver." "Kurt used to have fun with the fellows at night, throwing Charmin back and forth," says his grandfather, Otis Lingenfelter. "He'd tell the stock boys in the back that they'd one day see him playing professionally. They'd laugh at him, but he could throw a roll of toilet paper from one side of the store to another."

Warner had worked at the Hy-Vee for several months when he got a phone call from John Gregory, head coach of the Arena Football League's newest addition, the Iowa Barnstormers. Launched in 1987, the AFL had just expanded to 13 teams with the inclusion of Iowa in its 1995 schedule. The Barnstormers, who would play in Des Moines, were looking for a quarterback, and Gregory had just heard

Barnstormers fullback John Motten (No. 42) attempts to block as quarterback Kurt Warner (No. 13) eludes Arizona Rattlers defenders Hunkie Cooper, bottom, and Bob McMillen (No. 44) during first-half action in the ArenaBowl, the arena football championship game, in Phoenix on Monday, August 25, 1997.

Brenda's parents, who were tragically killed by a tornado.

Kurt and Brenda attend Muhammad Ali's Celebrity Fight Night in Phoenix, AZ, on March 28, 2009.

from Terry Allen, Northern Iowa's football coach at the time.

"I've got this quarterback who only played one year and was behind a guy who started three years," Allen told Gregory. "He had a good year and great game against Western Illinois." A tape of the game, in which Warner had passed for 356 yards and three touchdowns, was on Gregory's desk.

"Kurt and I had a couple conversations and he came for a workout," Gregory says. "I thought he looked good and had potential."

Warner had caught a few arena games on TV, and they weren't quite what he had in mind for a pro career. This was Ringling Brothers football, an indoor gridiron circus of eight players on each side darting about and colliding on carpets half the length and width of a normal field, bouncing off padded walls and occasionally over them into the laps of customers. All this amid goofy contests, halftime exhibitions, dance teams, mascots, cheerleaders, thunderous music, and harsh PA announcers hyping attendance for players who couldn't make it in the NFL.

The Barnstormers offered him $1,000 per game, an apartment in Des Moines, plus the chance to earn more money in the off-season with promotional work. What choice did he have? Making $44 a night at the Hy-Vee?

It took Warner some time to tailor his skills to the cramped dimensions of the field and chaotic pinball style of play. But after he figured it out and was all business in his determination to do so, the Arena Football League would never be the same again.

In three seasons he blistered defenses for 10,486 yards and 183 touchdowns—once throwing nine in one game. Twice Warner led the Barnstormers to the coveted ArenaBowl championship, and fans cheered him as "Houdini Warner" while he ducked and weaved, squirmed and spun away from clawing tacklers before loosing another of his breathtaking throws.

"He's a dodging kind of quarterback who moves around very nicely," says Tim Marcum, the Tampa Bay Storm coach who would become the most successful in AFL history with seven ArenaBowl titles. "He has a clock in his head, and he's patient with his surroundings. We knocked him around pretty good, but he's a tough guy. He'd stand in there and take it."

Gregory agrees. "He had a real quick delivery and still does, with a lot of zip on the ball. In the Arena League you get a lot of pressure in a very small space, and you have to get rid of the ball. That's why he's so good at raising up and throwing or using a three-step drop."

Of what the arena game taught him, Warner says, "Playing in a little cracker box, you've got to react quicker. The windows of opportunity are very narrow. You have to get back and throw as soon as your back foot hits the carpet."

In three seasons with the Barnstormers, the most money Warner earned was $65,000 with

Kurt Warner stands with his daughter Jesse directly after his Iowa Barnstormers jersey was retired.

Brenda questioned her own faith after her parents were killed.

incentives. Yet despite his soaring statistics and the NFL's need for quarterbacks, not one team attempted to sign him.

On Sunday night, April 14, 1996, Warner was watching television in his apartment in Des Moines. He had played in an exhibition game the night before in Moline, Illinois, and he was just nodding off about midnight when the phone rang. It was Brenda calling from Cedar Falls.

"Mom and Dad were killed in a tornado. I need you." Click. He tried to call her back three times, but the line was busy.

A week earlier Brenda's parents, Larry and Jenny Carney, had moved into the dream home they had built on the White River in Mountain View, Arkansas. Saturday, April 13, had been Larry's 54th birthday, and Brenda had talked to her father on Sunday. He had mentioned tornado warnings in the area, not unusual

in springtime, and said that even though Jenny had a headache, they were going to their new church that night to be baptized. He said they would call her when they returned home.

When the phone rang at 10:00 PM, Brenda thought it was her parents calling as promised. But it was her sister Kim.

That evening the Carneys had stayed home because of Jenny's headache, and about 7:30 PM two tornadoes collided above their roof. Their home vanished. Five neighbors were killed with them. The death of Brenda's father and mother would strike deep within her soul, to the very core of her belief in God.

Brenda Carney had been "born again" at age 12. During a Sunday night service at Sunny Side Temple in Waterloo, Iowa, she had risen from the pew and walked down to the altar to pray for forgiveness and ask Jesus to come into her heart. "I was saved that night," she said.

Kurt Warner had been raised a Catholic in Cedar Rapids. He attended Mass every Sunday and tried to be a good Christian. He tried to follow the Ten Commandments. He believed that if he was a good person, if he helped others and praised the Lord with his heart and mind, he had a shot at heaven.

Brenda's view was not so accommodating. She told Kurt he had to have a personal relationship with the lord, that he must first ask Jesus into his life. Quoting scripture, she insisted that no person earns salvation through good works, that all are sinners, and that the only way to be saved is through God's grace. "Your salvation is a gift from God," she said. "Just ask him. Jesus is your friend. He's here. You need him in your life every minute of every day."

Their disagreements grew heated.

Brenda was unyielding in her belief that Kurt still wasn't saved. He was just as convinced that his religious beliefs were personal, between him and his god, and quite frankly, they were none of her business. She said that if he had devoted his life to Christ, he would be out there telling people about him. He viewed that as implying he wasn't a Christian. "I didn't want to hear it," he said. "I didn't want any part of it. I still felt the way I was raised, and what I believed in, was enough."

In Des Moines, one of his Barnstormers teammates had started up a Bible group with a local pastor, and Warner had begun to attend the meetings. There would be no single moment when he felt he was born again, as she had been at 12. It was a gradual process, one that originated in Des Moines and evolved over a span of months. He didn't tell Brenda or anyone in his Bible group about the prayers he offered up for his salvation.

It was during the days and weeks after her desperate call to Des Moines that he sensed his life changing. He became her rock, keeping his own hurt to himself because she could not bear any more. He cared for Zach and Jesse Jo. He tried to answer their questions about what had happened to Grandpa and Grandma.

"I really began to feel the lord's presence in my life," Warner said. "I could just feel his peace all over me."

The dark irony was that as his faith began to deepen, Brenda began to question her own. Her parents? Swept away, never to be seen alive by her again.

"I don't have the answers to why my parents were killed," she said. "I could either go through it and not love God or go through it and love God. I don't understand why they died, but I know that he still loves me and that someday maybe it will make sense. Maybe it will be in heaven when I ask him."

Kurt used no words in his attempt to help Brenda through her grief. He just listened to her and tried to absorb some of her pain and anger in an effort to comfort her, especially after what had happened to Zachary four years earlier.

"There were times when I'd say, 'You just don't understand! You have both your parents!' And there were times when I was mad. I didn't understand how God could do this to me," Brenda said.

"But he didn't preach to me. He didn't preach to me like I'd been preaching to him two years before. He just listened. He held me. He was quiet and strong.

"It's exactly what I needed."

On October 11, 1997, Kurt and Brenda Warner were married in St. John's American Lutheran Church in Cedar Falls—the same church where a memorial service had been held for Larry and Jenny Carney 18 months earlier.

> The dark irony was that as his faith began to deepen, Brenda began to question her own. Her parents? Swept away, never to be seen alive by her again.
> "I don't have the answers to why my parents were killed," she said.

Kurt and Brenda were married on October 11, 1997, and continue to have a wonderful loving relationship to this day. Here he greets Brenda during a Rams game against the Cleveland Browns on October 24, 1999.

Scottish Claymores' Kerry Hicks attempts to tackle Amsterdam Admiral Warner.

4

NFL EUROPE &
EARLY RAMS

Every Sunday morning in Amsterdam, The Netherlands, he went to church. From the ferry on the Noordzeekanaal to Bookmark and Wallen, past the alleys and hotel rooms and the red lights glowing; past hookers beckoning from behind windows and the pimps in the doorways; past the sex museum, the sex shops, the peep shows, and hash bars in the streets—and through the doors of the church. "You take me," he prayed every Sunday morning. "You lead me. You help me."

Warner gets off a pass from the ground right before being tackled by Titans defenders.

In 1997, after leading the Iowa Barnstormers to a 12–2 record and second straight berth in the Arena Football League's championship game, Kurt Warner had reached the crossroads of his career. Now married, he, Brenda, and the children had moved into a new home in an upscale suburb of Des Moines. Their lives had come together at last, Zachary and Jesse Jo had made new friends, and his annual income was headed toward six figures.

But his chances of joining a National Football League team diminished. He had been cut by Green Bay. Tryouts with Cincinnati, Atlanta, and Tampa Bay had gone nowhere, as had discussions with several other NFL teams.

Earlier in the year he had been approached by the Amsterdam Admirals about playing in NFL Europe, a developmental league in which hundreds of aspirants compete in a 10-week season during the spring in hopes of being invited to an NFL training camp in August. "Kurt told me he really wanted to play in NFL Europe and have the NFL take a look at him," recalled Joe Clark, the Admirals' offensive coordinator. "But he was getting married later that year and had given his word to the Barnstormers he would play for them again that season."

The Admirals' head coach, Al Luginbill, was aware of Warner. On a scouting trip to California in 1996 he had gone to an Arena game in Anaheim to check out a former NFL lineman only to find himself transfixed by the No. 13 at quarterback for Iowa. "It was his accuracy and the way he handled himself," Luginbill recalled. "I said to myself, 'Whoa! Who is this guy?'"

At first Luginbill wondered why he was so enthralled by a 25-year-old who had been blown off by a half-dozen NFL

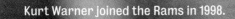
Kurt Warner joined the Rams in 1998.

Warner arrives for a Rams game with his wife Brenda and a bible in his hand.

teams. What made Luginbill think he saw something in Warner that everyone else had missed? "I researched him very carefully," Luginbill said. "I found nothing that made me doubt him. All he did was win."

Luginbill and Clark made Warner their No. 1 priority for the Admirals, and that fall Luginbill met him at the Cedar Falls YMCA, where he was working to supplement his Barnstormers income. They talked, and Warner said he would play on one condition: an NFL team had to try him out, sign him, and sponsor him overseas.

Luginbill called 13 NFL teams. One was interested.

> What made Luginbill think he saw something in Warner that everyone else had missed? "I researched him very carefully," Luginbill said. "I found nothing that made me doubt him. All he did was win."

"I had seen Kurt play," said Charley Armey, the St. Louis Rams director of player personnel, who had been tipped off by a coach of Warner's at Northern Iowa. "Mike Kolling was my first high school quarterback when I started coaching at Graceville, Minnesota," Armey said. "He told me the kid could play, and I went to watch him. He burned up the Arena League."

Warner got his workout with the Rams. "They liked him," Luginbill said. "They signed him and shipped him off to Amsterdam."

"Charley Armey is the best there is," Rams head coach Dick Vermeil would say.

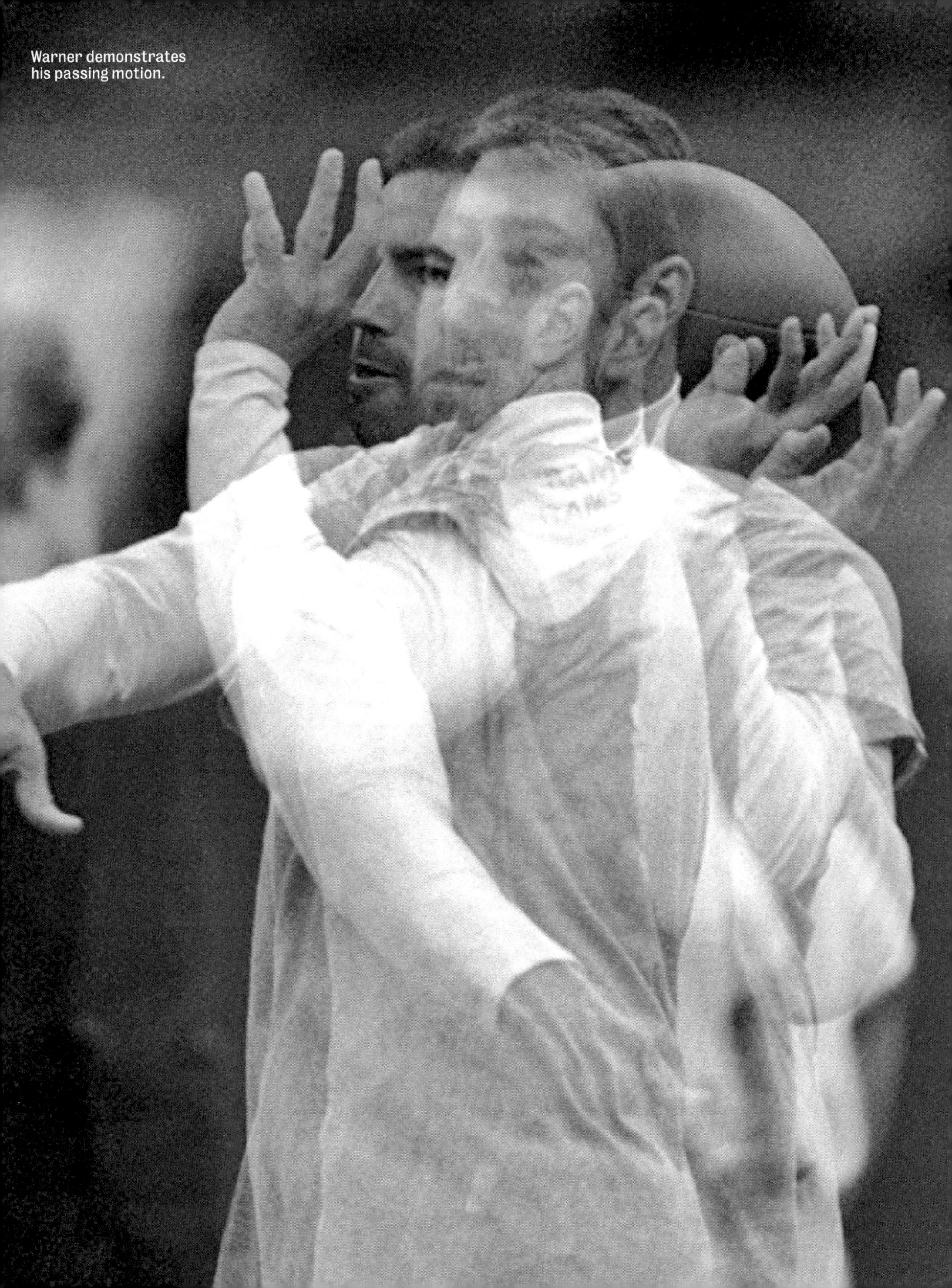

Warner demonstrates
his passing motion.

In his first game with the Rams, Warner completed four of 11 passes for 39 yards.

"When it comes to Kurt, Charley is the reason he's here."

Meanwhile, Joe Clark of the Admirals was working the familiar turf of his home state of Louisiana, where he'd been watching a fiery quarterback at little Louisiana-Lafayette named Jake Delhomme. Ignored in the 1996 NFL draft, Delhomme had signed as a free agent to quarterback the New Orleans Saints practice squad. "I really liked Jake," Clark said. "After the Saints signed him, we got them to allocate him to Amsterdam."

Now the Admirals had an intriguing quarterback competition. Both had played for small schools and had gone undrafted by the NFL. Both would be making $16,000 for the 10-game season. Warner, 26, was recently married with two small children and a third on the way back in Iowa; Delhomme, 23, was homesick for his wife-to-be back in Cajun country. Both were religious and spent a lot of time on the phone.

"You didn't go there to get rich," Delhomme said. "You went to play."

Neither knew or had even heard of the other until their first day on the practice field. After watching the other throw, each knew he would be challenged.

"No question Jake was a lot more talented than I was," Warner said. "He had the stronger arm, he moved better. He could make the big throws and the big plays a lot better. All I was hoping—no offense to Jake—was that he would make a few more mistakes so the coaches would give me a chance. Jake was a young kid who was going to get another chance. I was never going to get another chance."

"All I knew was that he was an Arena quarterback," Delhomme said. "But you could tell from the first practice that he

Brought in as the Rams' third-string quarterback, nobody could have foreseen that Warner would take the team to this Super Bowl victory over the Tennessee Titans.

was very accurate, a very heady quarterback. He had two kids and was starting to get up there. This was it for him."

Delhomme thought he won the starting job. In fact, he still does to this day and remembers being angry when Warner was named No. 1. According to Clark, Warner had an early advantage with his Arena experience. But in the final week of camp, Delhomme was closing fast.

"It was a really tough choice," Clark said.

Luginbill, who had worked hard to convince the Rams and Saints to allocate both to Amsterdam, said, "Kurt had played very successfully as a professional, regardless of what you may think of the Arena League," Luginbill said. "At that particular time, he was ahead of Jake. Jake doesn't like to hear that, but it was true."

Free of the confines of a football field 50 yards long, 85 feet wide, and surrounded by boundaries, Warner swept the Admirals to a 7–3 record and division title with a league-leading 2,101 yards passing for 15 touchdowns and 165 completions in 326 attempts. Twice he was named Offensive Player of the Week. "Amsterdam was about as different as it got for a guy from Iowa," he said. "But the thing that was most familiar to me was an outdoor field 100 yards long. I was finally back in real football."

His most profound demonstration came against the Barcelona Dragons, when Warner threw for 387 yards and an NFL Europe–record five touchdowns in a 41–28 victory. The headlines of the local paper blared, "Het verschil was vooral die ene man, quarterback Kurt Warner, bijgenaamd Houdini."

"I was a bit concerned at first how Kurt would adjust to a regular NFL field," Clark

Mike Martz talks to Warner on the sideline. Martz was named head coach of the Rams after the retirement of Dick Vermeil, who brought Warner onto the team in an effort to resurrect the failing franchise.

said. "But he told me the pass rush in the Arena League gets to the quarterback so fast that you learn how to get rid of the football quicker. He had a very strong arm, and he could rifle that ball in real tight spots. Kurt is built like a lumberjack, and he isn't afraid to hold on to the football until the very last second."

"He has everything you look for," gushed Luginbill. "Not just during a play, but in managing a team on the field. He has the same demeanor all the time. He's got strong faith in himself, and the bigger the situation, the better he plays."

Watching from the sideline was difficult

Both would be making $16,000 for the 10-game season. Warner, 26, was recently married with two small children and a third on the way back in Iowa; Delhomme, 23, was homesick for his wife-to-be back in Cajun country. "You didn't go there to get rich," Delhomme said. "You went to play."

for such a competitor as Delhomme, whose only start came when Warner missed one game with a strained shoulder.

"Here I am backing up a quarterback from the Iowa Barnstormers," Delhomme said. "How am I going to play in the NFL if I can't beat out an Arena quarterback?"

Which, of course, was precisely the point: intense exposure to Arena football worked to the benefit of a potential NFL quarterback, not against him.

Warner believed that Arena play had forced him to learn the short, crisp passing

Despite Warner's mediocre start with the Rams, there were many great things yet to come.

game and make decisions on the run. With the Admirals, he was able to put those techniques to the test on "the big field," as he called it. After Armey had flown to Amsterdam to see for himself, he told Warner over dinner one night, "You're doing some things better than any of the guys we've got back in St. Louis."

For Delhomme, the spring of 1998 in Amsterdam proved to be beneficial. A year later he returned to Europe and flourished with the Frankfurt Galaxy, earning his own shot in the NFL. As the Saints' backup quarterback in 1999, he watched as Warner rose to become the NFL's Most Valuable Player, then MVP of the Super Bowl. "It gave me great confidence," Delhomme said. "Hey, maybe I can play in this league too."

Three years later, Delhomme made his first NFL start. "After the game, the first message on the answering machine in my apartment was from Kurt Warner," he said. "That's the kind of guy he is." A few months later Delhomme quarterbacked Carolina to the Super Bowl.

"Only in America," said Luginbill. "You don't always get that opportunity to work with young men like those two guys."

When he learned of Warner's solitary treks through the red-light districts of Amsterdam to church every Sunday morning, it was Luginbill who suggested to his quarterback that he launch a series of prayer studies for his Admirals team-

> "He has everything you look for," gushed Luginbill. "Not just during a play, but in managing a team on the field. He has the same demeanor all the time. He's got strong faith in himself, and the bigger the situation, the better he plays."

mates. Warner did just that. Before long he was leading a bunch of them through the sordid streets of Bookmark and Sharee Wallen to church on Sunday.

Upon his return to St. Louis from Amsterdam, Armey presented his report on Warner to Dick Vermeil: "Accurate, poised, handles pressure, smart, pretty good arm, adequate mobility."

After his final game in Holland, a 26–23 victory over the Scottish Claymores, Warner said, "I feel that I've really picked up my game. Making good decisions, making all the different throws. It's enjoyable to go out and do what I love on the big field. It just seems like there's a lot of room out there."

"Every once in awhile a guy slips through the cracks," Armey said. "I look for this kid to do well. He's not doing any better than I thought he would do."

When other NFL teams started calling about Warner, all Armey would say was, "We have plans for him."

First, of course, Warner had to make the Rams' roster for 1998. The Rams' starting quarterback, Tony Banks, 25, had thrown for almost 6,000 yards his first two years in the NFL. His backup was veteran Steve Bono, 36. That left Warner to battle it out with Will Furrer, 30.

A fourth-round pick by the Chicago Bears in 1992, Furrer had appeared in only nine games in four years with four NFL teams. In 1996 and 1997, he too had played

for Amsterdam (it was his single-game team record of 384 yards passing that Warner had broken with 387 against Barcelona).

After being hired as head coach and president of football operations in 1997 to revive the moribund Rams, Vermeil had chosen Jerry Rhome as offensive coordinator. Rhome had coached Furrer in Houston and Arizona, and he suggested the Rams sign him to compete for the No. 3 job.

> Furrer brushed past him without a word. He knew. A few minutes later, it was official. Four long years of NFL rejection had vanished for Warner.

In St. Louis, Furrer went out of his way to be friendly and helpful to Warner; his knowledge of Rhome's system from Houston even accelerated Warner's grasp of the Rams' offense. But over the course of the next month, competition between the two became so close that the decision wouldn't be made the day before NFL's deadline for final roster cuts. Deep into the night the lights burned in a large conference room at Rams Park

Brenda cheers on her husband at a Rams game.

in suburban St. Louis. Rhome, of course, lobbied hard for Furrer. Mike White, Vermeil's top assistant, favored Warner. Vermeil was torn between the two quarterbacks so desperate for the job. Eventually the entire Rams coaching staff was called into the room.

When Warner arrived the next morning, Furrer brushed past him without a word. He knew. A few minutes later, it was official. Four long years of NFL rejection had vanished for Warner. In a private moment, Vermeil told him, "There's something special about you."

Later that day, Vermeil told the media, "He's very impressive. He gets back in the pocket and has a great feel for pass rushers. He finds throwing lanes instinctively. He throws awfully well and delivers it quickly. I think his only limitation is experience."

For Vermeil, 62, much was riding on this, his second season as the man with

full authority (and a three-year $10 million contract) to resurrect the Rams. He had pulled it off before, infusing new life into the moribund Philadelphia Eagles in the late 1970s and taking them to the Super Bowl in 1980. Three years later he retired, self-diagnosed with "burnout," and for 14 years managed to avoid the demons of the work to which he was addicted. But when a dear friend, Rams owner Georgia Frontiere, came calling a third time, Vermeil couldn't turn her down.

The Rams, 7–9 and 6–10 in St. Louis since moving from Los Angeles in 1995, slid even further to 5–11 in Vermeil's first year. Whispers were that he was "out of touch" with the new breed of NFL player and that the game itself had "passed him by."

Going into their sixth game of the 1998 season, at Miami, the Rams were 2–3. Each of their defeats was by seven points or less. The offense was averaging a robust 25.8 points per game. After a 14–0 loss to the Dolphins, however, the Rams collapsed. They were 2–9 in their last 11 games, averaging only 14.2 points per game. Star wideout Isaac Bruce started quickly and then missed most of the

Despite the many lows in his life and the difficulty he had breaking into the NFL, the Rams opened the door to the happiness Kurt and Brenda so deeply deserved. The happy Warner family is pictured here with former Rams coach Dick Vermeil.

season with a hamstring injury. Greg Hill had 240 yards rushing and four touchdowns to lead the NFL after the first two games, but his season ended with a broken leg in the third. Tony Banks threw twice as many interceptions as touchdown passes before sustaining a season-ending knee injury in the next-to-last game of the year.

Late in the afternoon of Sunday, December 27, 1998, the scoreboard clock in San Francisco's Candlestick Park glowed 3:38. The 49ers had just scored again to

> ...the Rams third-string quarterback removed his headset, picked up his blue helmet with the curled yellow horns on the sides, and jogged onto the lush green turf and into his first game in the National Football League.

lead the Rams 38–19, when the voice of Dick Vermeil crackled over the headset, "Kurt, you want to go in?"

With that, the Rams' third-string quarterback removed his headset, picked up his blue helmet with the curled yellow horns on the sides, and jogged onto the lush green turf and into his first game in the National Football League. He completed four of 11 passes for 39 yards.

No touchdowns. No surprises. They were yet to come.

Warner signs autographs for Rams fans.

Warner celebrates the Rams' 23–16 victory over the Tennessee Titans in Super Bowl XXXIV on January 30, 2000.

· 5 ·
ASCENSION WITH THE RAMS

Ten days after the Rams' 12th and final defeat of the 1998 NFL season, head coach Dick Vermeil was in the office of team president John Shaw in Los Angeles. Their meeting lasted five hours, and according to Vermeil, "went about as well as it could go for only winning four games all year."

Things had not been going very well since Vermeil was hired in 1997 as the Rams' head coach and president of player operations. The Rams, 13–19 in the two years before Vermeil arrived, were 9–23 with him in control. Rumors of a possible team mutiny had surfaced over his marathon practice sessions. Quarterback Tony Banks had skipped practice one day to care for his sick cat. And now four prominent Rams players had just boycotted Vermeil's final team meeting of the season, an act he viewed as a "shot in the back."

Although nobody said so, the sense was that if the Rams did not show dramatic improvement in the third year of Vermeil's five-year contract, he would not be back for the fourth.

Vermeil never doubted that Warner could step in and do the job left vacant by the injured Trent Green.

Trent Green was selected as the Rams' quarterback after achieving 3,441 yards and 23 touchdowns for Washington in 1998.

John Shaw was a lawyer, not a football man. But after devoting considerable thought to the plight of the Rams, Shaw had some suggestions for his coach to consider. First, hire a new offensive coordinator. Next, find a good quarterback. Finally, clear the locker room of the malcontents and get some players in there with talent and character. And by the way, ease up on the practice field. Your players might reward you for it. Both agreed that the Rams should be more aggressive in their pursuit of talent.

Within weeks the Rams hired the most daring offensive mind in the NFL—Mike Martz—from the Washington Redskins. Soon to follow was free-agent quarterback Trent Green, who had flourished under Martz in Washington (3,441 yards and 23 touchdown passes in 1998). "Trent is a complete quarterback," Martz said. "He sees the field well, makes good decisions, doesn't panic, is an accurate passer, and he has no ego." Green, who had in fact grown up in the St. Louis area, signed a $16.5 million four-year contract with the Rams.

In February the Rams left Warner unprotected in the draft to stock the Cleveland Browns' return to the NFL. Charley Armey called the decision "a foolish gamble," because for only $10,000 the Browns could bring him in for a closer look. Warner understood, saying, "I knew where I was and where I came from."

> Clearly the Rams had been "aggressive" in their off-season acquisitions, and the result of such bold moves and brash outlays of cash was a huge spike in interest for the 1999 season. At the core of the anticipation rush was Green, who was directing Martz's take-no-prisoners attack like a field commander.

With little film of Warner available, and quarterback Tim Couch of Kentucky their likely No. 1 pick in the college draft, the Browns decided not to "muddy the waters" with Warner.

"I didn't think they'd waste a pick on me," Warner said.

"We were lucky Cleveland didn't do their homework," Armey said.

By now the Rams had also invested $19 million in Adam Timmerman, a free-agent offensive guard from the Green Bay Packers. They spent more millions by making star receiver Torry Holt of North Carolina State their No. 1 choice in the NFL draft. And in August, they sent two garden-variety draft picks to the Indianapolis Colts for holdout All-Pro running back/receiver Marshall Faulk, then signed him for $45 million. "This is by far the biggest contract in Rams history," Shaw said. "We really expect Marshall to make a significant contribution."

Clearly the Rams had been "aggressive" in their off-season acquisitions, and the result of such bold moves and brash outlays of cash was a huge spike in interest for the 1999 season. At the core of the anticipation rush was Green, who was directing Martz's take-no-prisoners attack like a field commander.

Late in the first half of the Rams' third preseason game, against the San Diego

Chargers in the TWA Dome, Green had already thrilled the hometown crowd with a perfect 11-for-11 display for 166 yards and a gorgeous 52-yard touchdown strike to Isaac Bruce. His preseason stats: 28 of 32, 406 yards, two touchdowns.

Now, as Green retreated to pass one final time, San Diego's Rodney Harrison bore in on a blitz from the left corner. Faulk stepped up to knock Harrison off stride, and as Green put the ball in the air, Harrison rolled awkwardly into his left leg and firmly planted foot.

Green went down as if he'd been shot.

As a doctor and trainers hustled out to where Green lay writhing and groaning in pain, the stadium fell silent. On the sideline, Isaac Bruce ripped off his helmet, knelt, and pounded the turf with his fist. Long minutes passed. Finally there was a smattering of applause from the crowd and tears welling in the eyes of Green's teammates as he was carted off the field holding his left knee, three ligaments shredded, his season over before it began. In the hours after the game, the franchise was in disarray.

Shaw was stunned.

Vermeil was disoriented over a decision to be made, heartbroken for Green.

Armey looked at Vermeil. "What are we going to do?"

"Kurt's our quarterback. I have confidence he can do the job."

"What if he flops?"

"Some people can handle it. Some can't."

Armey glowed inside. He reflected much later, "Some, like Kurt Warner, combat pressure with supreme confidence. It's his defining trait, even if it is hard to comprehend how someone so raw comes by it in such abundance. When I flew over to NFL Europe and watched him play with the Admirals, I took him to dinner. He looked me right in the eye and said, 'If I get the opportunity, I'll be your quarterback.'"

By the afternoon after Green's injury, everybody had said all the right things.

Vermeil said, "We will rally around Kurt Warner, and we will play good football."

Warner said, "I'm going to be as successful as Trent would have been in the exact same situation."

> "There wasn't anyone thinking Kurt Warner was going to be the answer," he said. "We were hardly thinking he should be on the squad. But when Trent Green got hurt, we were going to drop Kurt Warner in there and find out. Once he had the responsibility, the guy went crazy."

Bruce told Warner, "Just drive the car. Steer the car, be the eyes. We'll be the wheels."

In the final preseason game, a 17–6 victory over the Detroit Lions in the Pontiac Silverdome, Warner started out a little shaky, then finished solid, capable, and poised. On the sideline, the coaches looked at each other.

A week later in the TWA Dome, in his first NFL start, Warner passed for 309 yards and three touchdowns in a 27–10 victory against a Baltimore Ravens team renowned for its fierce defense. The following week the Rams crushed the defending

An injured Trent Green uses a crutch
after being injured by Rodney Harrison
of the Chargers.

In his first NFL start, Warner passed
for 309 yards and three touchdowns.

By the afternoon after Trent Green's injury, Kurt Warner was officially the Rams' new quarterback.

Warner set a record by achieving the most touchdown passes by a quarterback in his first four games.

NFC champion Atlanta Falcons 35–7 with Warner throwing for three more scores. Then came the Bengals at Cincinnati, where another trio of scoring passes doomed the Bengals 38–10.

Former NFL coach John Ralston, who had been a consultant for the Rams in training camp, recalled what transpired. "There wasn't anyone thinking Kurt Warner was going to be the answer," he said. "We were hardly thinking he should be on the squad. But when Trent Green got hurt, we were going to drop Kurt Warner in there and find out. Once he had the responsibility, the guy went crazy."

The San Francisco 49ers was the next team to visit the TWA Dome. Bitter California rivals since their first match in 1950, this Los Angeles–San Francisco saga had grown in intensity during the 1970s, when both teams were regular competitors for the NFC West title. Due primarily to teams that won five Super Bowl championships between 1982 and 1995, the 49ers had assumed the upper hand in the rivalry, beating the Rams 17 times in a row since 1990. The San Franciscans were never shy about celebrating their dominance either. Even after their geographical rivals had moved to St. Louis, the 49ers still mocked and taunted them as "the same old Rams."

October 11, 1999, is a day that will live forever in the annals of Rams-49ers warfare. Before a raucous standing-room-only crowd of 65,872 spectators, Kurt Warner torched the 49ers with nine completions in nine attempts for 177 yards and three touchdowns for a 21–3 Rams advantage at the end of the first quarter. And the Rams never ceased firing until one minute remained in the 42–20 rout, when backup quarterback Paul Justin twice took a knee at the 49ers' 1-yard line.

As the *New York Times* would report, "It was similar to an old schoolyard tussle where the loser's arm is bent behind his back and the winner demands that he yell and spell u-n-c-l-e!"

"There was no need to try to score again," Vermeil said. "I think they knew that.

"When they came off the field, I could see in their eyes that they were kind of baffled," noted Rams linebacker Mike Jones. In fact the 49ers, 3–1 coming into the game, would lose their next seven in a row and 10 of their last 11.

"This is my sixth year here, and I've been a part of a lot of those 17 losses to the 49ers," said Rams safety Keith Lyle. "This locker room was celebrating because we earned this game. A lot of guys were almost in tears."

Indeed, the Rams defense had been an assault force throughout, picking off three 49ers passes along the way. Not to be upstaged, Rams special teams brought down the thunder with a 97-yard kickoff return for a touchdown.

> Warner? His five touchdown passes brought his season total to 14—the most in NFL history by a quarterback in his first four games. All he seemed to be lacking were some fresh quotes for the horde of national media beginning to descend upon him.

In a private moment, Dick Vermeil told Warner, "There's something special about you."

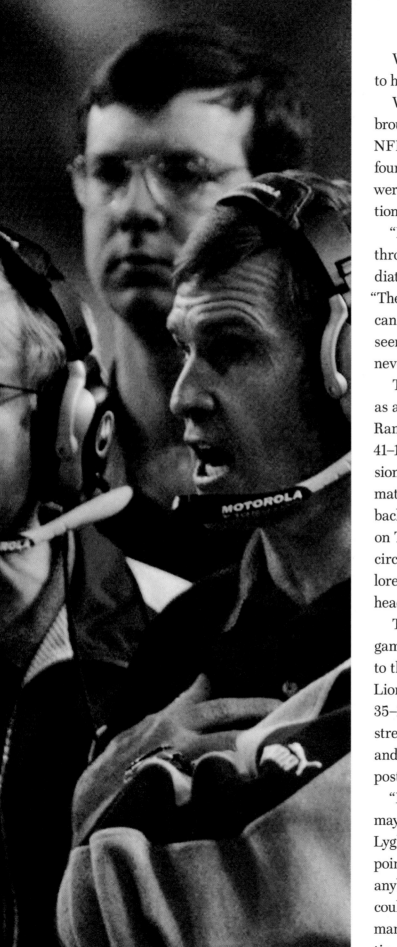

When his players handed the game ball to him, Vermeil called it "a meaningful gift."

Warner? His five touchdown passes brought his season total to 14—the most in NFL history by a quarterback in his first four games. All he seemed to be lacking were some fresh quotes for the horde of national media beginning to descend upon him.

"I always felt I could make the long throws, the short throws, and the intermediate ones, and I made them today," he said. "The only way you can find out if a player can play is if he plays. The league hadn't seen much of me in a football game. I've never had the chance to play until now."

The San Francisco game would serve as a metaphor for what was to come. The Rams ripped the Falcons again, this time 41–13 in Atlanta, then shelled the expansionist Browns 34–3. With its myriad formations, man-in-motion and ever-shifting backs and receivers, "the Greatest Show on Turf" showered the sports world with circus catches and gridiron acrobatics galore. "Who is this Guy?" *Sports Illustrated* headlined a cover story on Warner.

The Rams dropped back-to-back road games by a total of seven points (21–24 to the Tennessee Titans and 27–31 to the Lions), then bombed the Carolina Panthers 35–10 to launch a seven-game winning streak (23–7, 43–12, 34–21, 30–14, 31–10, and 34–12) before a don't-get-hurt-for-the-postseason loss at Philadelphia (31–38).

"I thought we could have a decent club, maybe win 10 games," cornerback Todd Lyght recalled. "But we're at the halfway point at 6–2, and we thought we could beat anybody. That's when the team knew we could get this thing done. There were so many growing periods where we just continued to get better and believe in ourselves."

Warner manages to unload a pass as he is brought down in Super Bowl XXXIV against the Tennessee Titans.

Their regular-season statistics were astonishing. Snapping a streak of nine straight losing seasons, the Rams averaged 33 points per game for a total of 526—third-most in NFL history. Warner completed 325 of 499 passes for 4,353 yards and 41 touchdowns, joining Dan Marino as the only quarterback in NFL history to throw for 40 or more touchdowns in a single season. Bruce caught 77 passes for 1,165 yards and 12 scores. Faulk scampered for 1,381 yards and seven touchdowns, caught 87 passes for 1,048 yards and five touchdowns, and set a new NFL record for total offense with 2,429 yards.

The Rams' defense flourished too, tying for the NFL's best in sacks (57), leading it in average rushing yardage allowed per game (74), and returning seven interceptions for touchdowns.

In one of the most remarkable turnabouts in history—4–12 in 1998 to 13–3 in 1999—the Rams lost three games by a scant 14 points and were 8–0 at the TWA Dome, where they prevailed by an average score of 35–10. With the stellar seasons of both Warner and Faulk before them, voters thought long and hard before Warner edged his teammate as the league's Most Valuable Player.

"If ever I got the opportunity, I could be successful," Warner said. "Through the times I worked in the supermarket and played in Arena football, I never lost sight of that. That's what it's all about. Believing

> "If ever I got the opportunity, I could be successful," Warner said. "Through the times I worked in the supermarket and played in Arena football, I never lost sight of that. That's what it's all about. Believing in yourself."

in yourself. I just went out and did what I expected myself to do, things I've been doing the last few years. It just happens that people who hadn't seen me do those things before got to see me do them this year."

The NFC West title game brought the Minnesota Vikings to the TWA Dome, where 35 unanswered points early in the second half propelled the Rams to a 49–37 triumph. The Tampa Bay Buccaneers were another story in the NFC Championship Game. Keying on Faulk and ultimately holding him to 51 yards rushing, the Bucs were defending a hard-earned 6–5 advantage with five minutes to play.

Then, with the ball at the Bucs' 30-yard line, Warner lofted a pass into the end zone to Ricky Proehl, who caught the ball with one hand and secured it to his body while tumbling to the turf. The touchdown pass—for an 11–6 victory—sent the Rams to the Georgia Dome in Atlanta for Super Bowl XXXIV against the Tennessee Titans.

Like the Rams, the Titans were labeled a team of destiny. Indeed, the "Music City Miracle" that got them to Atlanta is one of the most memorable finishes in NFL postseason history.

After Steve Christie's magnificent 51-yard field goal had given the Buffalo Bills a 16–15 lead in the AFC Championship Game in Nashville, only 16 seconds remained on the clock when the Bills kicked off to the Titans. But then Frank Wycheck, upon fielding the kickoff, tossed a lateral to teammate Kevin Dyson, who raced 75 yards for the winning touchdown.

Early in the big game, Warner and the Rams moved the ball with consistency against the Titans. Even so, Warner was being pounded by Tennessee's defensive front and, after settling for field goals instead of touchdowns, the Rams led by only 9–0 at halftime.

In the third quarter Warner finally found Torry Holt for a touchdown and a 16–0 Rams advantage. But then Steve McNair drove the Titans 66 yards for a touchdown. A two-point conversion failed. The Titans held the Rams and quickly scored again, making the score 16–13. More than 70,000 spectators and a worldwide audience of tens of millions sensed forthcoming drama, and when Al Del Greco's 43-yard field goal tied the game at 16 with 2:12 remaining, the stage was set for a classic finish.

Following the kickoff, the Rams took possession at their own 27. In Warner's words, the idea was to "get a big one right off the bat"—Bruce on a "go route."

"We'd called it earlier, and Isaac had beaten his guy," Warner said. "Maybe they weren't expecting it."

"We didn't want to go to overtime," Bruce said. "They'd been in man-to-man coverage all day. There was no trickery. Kurt just had to make sure he got the ball to me."

As Warner dropped back, Bruce broke free. But suddenly, Titans defensive end Jevon Kearse was in Warner's face—again! Kearse sent Warner sprawling, but not before he got off a desperate pass to Bruce. The ball was wobbly and short, but Bruce adjusted beautifully, returning a few steps to cradle it in his arms, then racing off on a 73-yard touchdown strike.

"All I saw were bodies everywhere," Warner said. "The crowd was roaring."

Rams 23, Titans 16. What a finish!

Not quite.

Moments later, McNair was scrambling for time deep in Rams territory. Time enough to deliver a 20-yard beauty to the "Miracle Man"—Dyson—at the Rams' 6-yard line.

Timeout, Tennessee!

On what would be the final play of this enthralling finish, McNair rifled the ball to Dyson on a slant with only Rams linebacker Mike Jones in his path to the end zone. As Jones' arms gathered around him, Dyson lunged forward, stabbing the ball with one hand toward the goal line.

"When he got his hands on me, I thought I'd break the tackle," Dyson said. "But he slid down to my foot, like you're supposed to, and made a great play. I realized as soon as I stretched out and was going down that I didn't get the point of the ball over the goal line."

"I just grabbed him, held on and fell down," Jones said. "When I looked up, the clock was zero-zero."

> The ball was wobbly and short, but Bruce adjusted beautifully, returning a few steps to cradle it in his arms, then racing off on a 73-yard touchdown strike. "All I saw were bodies everywhere," Warner said. "The crowd was roaring."

Though Warner played well, the Rams simply could not defeat the Patriots in Super Bowl XXXVI.

For his role in the victory—24 completions in 46 attempts for 414 yards and two touchdowns—Warner was named the game's MVP. As he reflected on what had transpired in the previous five months, he couldn't help but contrast his status then and now. "At that time it wasn't very realistic to think I'd be the starter in a Super Bowl game," he said. "They were still trying to figure out if I was good enough to be the backup."

Three days later, Vermeil tearfully announced that he was retiring as head coach of the Rams. In paying tribute to his players, he said, "They know how I feel about them, and maybe more important, I know how they feel about me." When asked why he had not taken more time to ponder his decision, Vermeil noted that his successor would soon be required to make some key decisions regarding the 2000 roster. "I don't want to cut the squad," he said. "These are my guys." (A year later, admitting he made "a mistake" by retiring so quickly, Vermeil was named head coach of the Kansas City Chiefs. Among his first moves was to acquire Trent Green to be his No. 1 quarterback.)

In 2000, Mike Martz's first year as head coach of the Rams, the defense failed miserably. Despite the return of 10 starters, the defense would yield an average of 30 points per game and skid from sixth-best in the NFL to 23rd. But the offense was lethal as ever. Going into their October 22 game at Kansas City, the Rams were 6–0,

> As he reflected on what had transpired in the previous five months, he couldn't help but contrast his status then and now. "At that time it wasn't very realistic to think I'd be the starter in a Super Bowl game..."

averaging 44 points per game, and Warner had thrown for more than 300 yards in each of them.

Against the Chiefs, the Rams lost their first game 54–34 and Warner for the next five games with a hairline fracture of the pinkie finger on his right hand. The following week, for the first time since he'd been carried from the field of the TWA Dome, Trent Green was the Rams' starting quarterback in a 34–24 victory at San Francisco.

"That start against the 49ers meant so much to me," Green said. "It meant the four surgeries and all the rehab I'd gone through was worth it."

While Warner was sidelined, Green completed 60 percent of his passes for 2,063 yards and 16 touchdowns. Warner finished with 3,429 yards and 21 touchdowns in 11 games. At season's end, the two had combined for 5,232 net passing yards—a new NFL record.

The Rams were eliminated from 2000 postseason play in a 31–24 loss to the New Orleans Saints.

Reflecting upon what might have been in his lost season of 1999, Green said, "It took me six years to reach that point. I finally felt like I had a team of my own, I proved to myself I could play in this league. Then to watch somebody do all the things I had aspired to do, and do the things I had hoped to do, it just gave me more motivation.

"That night changed the direction of my life and my career. It changed the direction of Kurt's life and his career."

In 2001 the arrival of defensive coordinator Lovie Smith from the Falcons provided a vastly improved defense for the Rams. And that, combined with another season of offensive fireworks, propelled the Rams to a 14–2 record and their second division title in three years. In winning his second league MVP award in three years, Warner completed 375 of 546 passes for 4,830 yards, 36 touchdowns, and a glowing 101.4 quarterback rating for the season.

At the same time, Faulk lived up to every expectation with John Shaw's 1999 announcement of his $45 million contract. In those three years, Faulk carried 766 times for 4,122 yards (5.4 per carry) and 37 touchdowns rushing. He also caught 251 passes for 2,643 yards (10.5 yards per reception) and 22 touchdowns. He was the first running back ever to gain 2,000 yards in four consecutive seasons. He was voted All-Pro all three seasons.

The Rams averaged 31.3 points a game, including the playoffs, and with eight new starters on defense, the team improved from 31st in points allowed in 2000 to seventh in 2001. After winning their first six games, the Rams bounced back from a loss to the Saints to win two straight, and after their loss to the Buccaneers they completed the season with six straight victories. They were 8–0 on the road.

In the NFC West title game, the Rams

> The Rams were 14-point favorites against the New England Patriots, and deservedly so. In fact, Faulk said it best when he intoned, "The only team that can beat us is us." What was so shocking was that the Rams went out and did just that.

demolished the Packers 45–17. In the NFC Championship Game, the Eagles' defense—the NFL's best—proved to be a major challenge. The Eagles led 17–13 at halftime, but Warner directed an attack that held the ball for all but five plays in the third quarter and scored twice to seize the lead. In the fourth quarter, Faulk tormented the Eagles for another score in the 29–24 triumph that sent the Rams to New Orleans and their second Super Bowl in three years.

The Rams were 14-point favorites against the New England Patriots, and deservedly so. In fact, Faulk said it best when he intoned, "The only team that can beat us is us." What was so shocking was that the Rams went out and did just that.

With the Rams leading 3–0 in the first quarter, Warner dropped back to pass from his 39-yard line when Patriots linebacker Mike Vrabel was honing in like a heat-seeking missile. Just before Vrabel arrived, Warner unloaded a pass directly into the hands of Pats cornerback Ty Law, who sped 47 yards down the sideline for a 7–3 New England advantage.

Then, with the Rams at their 15 with less than two minutes remaining in the first half, Warner fired deep over the middle to Ricky Proehl, who lost the ball when he was jarred by Antwan Harris. His teammate, Terrell Buckley, seized the loose ball and returned it 15 yards to the

Rams' 40. Five plays later, David Patten made a leaping catch of Tom Brady's eight-yard pass for a 14–3 New England lead.

"He put a helmet on the ball," Proehl would say. "Everybody fumbles. I'm human."

Incredibly, despite St. Louis' advantages in total yards (184–117), passing yards (131–60), offensive plays (34–26), and time of possession (16:40 to 13:20), that was the score at halftime. "It wasn't a matter of execution," Faulk would say. "It was a matter of taking care of the ball."

Baffling the Rams were the five, six, and sometimes even seven defensive backs Patriots coach Bill Belichick was employing to slow "the Greatest Show on Turf." As Law noted, "They say it's the best track team in the National Football League, but I never saw anybody win a 100-yard dash with someone standing in front of him."

To capitalize on New England's concentration of defensive backs, the Rams turned to running the ball. Faulk gained a solid 30 yards in four tries. On third down, however, Warner's pass missed Holt and was snatched out of the air by Otis Smith, who returned it 30 yards to the St. Louis 32. Three plays later, Adam Vinatieri's 37-yard field goal made it 17–3.

Early in the fourth quarter, the Rams responded with a drive inside the Patriots' 32-yard line for the first time in the game. On fourth-and-goal from the 2, Warner's sneak completed a 12-play, 73-yard drive that pulled the Rams to 17–10 with 9:31 remaining.

The Rams' defense rose up to halt the Patriots, and after taking possession at his

own 45, Warner's 26-yard pass to Proehl tied the game at 17–17.

Only 1:30 remained in regulation. A second classic finish for the Rams? The first sudden-death overtime in Super Bowl history?

It was not to be. With no timeouts and 1:21 remaining, Brady calmly led the Patriots on a nine-play 53-yard drive that set up Vinatieri's 48-yard field goal that split the goalposts with 0:00 showing on the clocks.

"A lot of bookies are probably mad at us right now, but we don't give a damn," Law shouted. "We're the champs."

"We shocked the world, but we didn't shock ourselves," said Vinatieri.

"The only team that could beat us was us, and we did," said Faulk. "We turned the ball over three times, and you can't do that. When you think about what happened here, it's just a case of they made more plays than we did. That's how you lose."

"When it came time to step up and make some plays, we didn't do it," defensive coordinator Lovie Smith said. "You've got to be able to stop them at the end."

The Patriots had defended masterfully against Faulk, who finished with only 76 yards in 17 carries—and only five carries in the second half.

Although Warner completed 26 of 48 passes for 365 yards and a touchdown, he was intercepted twice, one for a Patriots touchdown.

"For a long time," said St. Louis defensive tackle Tyoka Jackson, "this is going to be very painful."

> Only 1:30 remained in regulation. A second classic finish for the Rams? The first sudden-death overtime in Super Bowl history?

·6·
ENDINGS & NEW BEGINNINGS

Warner holds up his New York Giants jersey at a press conference announcing his signing with the team on June 3, 2004, two days after he was released by the Rams.

It was as if the rest of the NFL had just had it with the St. Louis Rams. Losing by a thousand cuts every Sunday. Puffy and purpled from all those float-like-a-butterfly-sting-like-a-bee sorties. Torched by 30 or more points in a game and knowing it could have been worse.

That's why they just tore one big page from New England's game plan after the Patriots marched into New Orleans for Super Bowl XXXIV and tore down every damn tent of what used to be the Greatest Show on Turf.

Smash-mouth, snot-nosed, take-names football, that's what it was. Worked in the Big Easy. Make it work anywhere.

Warner was released by the Rams in 2004 after Marc Bulger arrived on the team and seemed to be the better quarterback.

Eight months later it worked at Mile High Stadium in Denver, where the Broncos belted the Rams 23–16. "This game was for those who are used to getting physical," declared Denver's Trevor Pryce.

"They took the fight to us pretty good," said Rams coach Mike Martz. "They shook us up a bit."

The New York Giants brought more of the same the next week in a 26–21 victory over the Rams at the TWA Dome. "I made too many mistakes," lamented Warner, who managed only 266 yards passing and was intercepted twice. "I lost the game for this team. I didn't get it done."

Next was a *Monday Night Football* date in Tampa against the Buccaneers, who traditionally had laid the leather to the Rams. "We make mistakes we're not good enough to overcome," Martz sighed after the Bucs prevailed 26–14.

Warner was intercepted four more times. "I'm going to take this on my shoulders and keep swinging," he said.

During a 13–10 loss to the Dallas Cowboys at the TWA Dome, Warner was blitzed and fell awkwardly on his right hand as his errant pass was picked off. Unlike his injury to the same finger two years earlier, this was a compound fracture that would require eight to 10 weeks to recover from after surgery.

"I'm not believing that one bit," Warner snapped. "We've got too good of a team to believe that. I'm going to be back just in time to take us into the playoffs."

"He's very upset, but that's life," Martz said. "There's nothing you can do about it."

Coming into the 2002 season, the defending NFC champions had been considered capable of returning to the Super Bowl for

Warner and the Giants surprised the football world by winning five of the first seven games after Warner joined the team.

After achieving greatness with the Rams and seeming bound for the Pro Football Hall of Fame, Warner began to be ineffective.

Despite Warner's ambitious beginning in his first seven games with the Giants, Eli Manning (right) was picked over Warner (left) to start the remaining games of the season.

the third time in four years. Now 0–4 after their worst start in 39 years, the first NFL team ever to score 500 points three seasons in a row was averaging 15 per game. After a fifth consecutive defeat the following week in San Francisco, Marc Bulger, a talented rookie quarterback, stepped in to lead the Rams to five straight victories and level their record at 5–5.

Warner returned to start again, but in visits to Washington and Philadelphia he was ineffectual, twice losing as a result of fumbles, fluttering passes, and three interceptions that were returned for touch-downs. "Crazy things happened," he said after the 13–6 loss to the Eagles. "It's frus-trating to come away not doing what you needed to do to win. It hurts."

Martz had suspected that at some point in the Redskins game Warner had hurt his hand again. Originally, doctors thought it was a deep bruise to the palm of Warner's hand, but the day after the Philadelphia game X-rays revealed a hairline fracture of the fifth metacarpal of the hand. Warner was placed on injured reserve, ending his 2002 season. "You never want to be where you're not going to play the rest of the year, but it's probably the best thing," he said. "I want to be able to do the things I'm capa-ble of doing. In the back of my mind, I be-lieved there was an outside chance I could."

For a world-class professional athlete, this was the worst of times. Appearing bound for the NFL Hall of Fame, twice the league's MVP, and once MVP in the Super Bowl, now Warner had been 0–6 as

> "I made too many mistakes," lamented Warner, who managed only 266 yards passing and was intercepted twice. "I lost the game for this team. I didn't get it done."

a starting quarterback. His numbers were abysmal: 144 completions in 220 attempts for 1,431 yards and three touchdowns with 11 interceptions. Eight fumbles, four of them lost. A quarterback rating of 67.4 (after 103.4 the year before). His skills had eroded dramatically; no longer was he poised and decisive.

He had not won a game as a starter since the 29–24 victory over the Eagles in the 2001 NFC Championship Game. That was more than 18 months before. Including the loss to New England in the Super Bowl, his record as a starter was 0–8.

Even so, he would rise above this. In an interview with *Christian Reader* magazine, he said, "In the fickle world of professional sports, where it's such a what-have-you-done-for-me-lately type business, I heard, 'You're too old. Your career's over. You'll never be back. It's all your fault.' There were times when it appeared that there was a spirit of division that was trying to come into the team. As difficult as it was on the field, it was that great off the field. My spiritual growth was probably at an all-time high. Every time I prayed and got into the Word, God just spoke to me. It was the greatest year of my life because of the spiritual growth that I went through."

Tight end Ernie Conwell of the New Orleans Saints, a close friend and former teammate of Warner, noticed this too. "Circumstances weren't dictating his value as a man and his attitude on life," Conwell told the magazine. "His walk with Christ grew stronger. If you look at his history,

In 2005—after leaving the Giants and with few NFL teams interested in him—Warner signed with the Arizona Cardinals.

every time he's been challenged, he's thrived. I have no doubt he'll come back."

Throughout the winter, spring, and summer of 2003, the Rams' quarterback situation simmered on the St. Louis sports scene. Warner, the former All-Pro? Bulger, the accomplished youngster? At last, Martz chose Warner to start the September 7 opener against the New York Giants at Giants Stadium.

It was a debacle for Warner, both personally and professionally. Under constant siege by the Giants' defensive front in the 23–13 defeat, Warner was manhandled into six fumbles and sacked another half-dozen times. Five times he was stripped of the ball in the first half, once for a New York touchdown.

As his Rams teammates boarded the buses and departed the stadium, Warner lay on a stretcher in the trainers' room with a severe headache, nausea, and a concussion. He would be held overnight at Cornell Medical Center for observation and neurological examinations. Later that night it was announced that a CAT scan and X-rays of his head and neck were negative.

"He got whacked on the head pretty good," Martz said of one particular sack in the first quarter. "We couldn't figure out why he was having such a hard time getting plays in. Right after that sack, he was hearing [the play], but he wasn't sorting it out. I didn't know what was going on. I thought we had a [wireless] communication problem."

When he complained of headaches at halftime, Warner was examined by team physician Bernard Garfinkel. "He felt fine [in the second half], and I talked to him several times in the third quarter," Garfinkel said. "He didn't start feeling bad in the locker room until after he got dressed. We decided to get a CAT scan and watch him overnight."

Martz said he wasn't informed of Warner's headaches until the start of the third quarter, when the doctors told him to be ready to play. "He just wasn't himself," Martz said. "He looked confused when you gave him a play. I shouldn't have played him. In retrospect, I regret playing him."

Warner passes the ball during second-quarter action against the Seattle Seahawks on September 25, 2005.

Warner pulls off an exceptional performance with the Cardinals, leading the team to a 29–24 victory over the San Francisco 49ers On November 10, 2008.

It was the last game Warner would ever start for the St. Louis Rams. As Bulger quarterbacked the Rams to a 12–3 record and berth in the playoffs, Warner contributed from the sideline.

Released on June 1, 2004, Warner was signed two days later by the Giants. They had just drafted a future star, Eli Manning, and Warner would be New York's starting quarterback that fall while mentoring Manning for the day he would become his successor.

"Kurt is a two-time league MVP who has taken his team to two Super Bowls and won one," said the Giants' new coach, Tom Coughlin. "He will work with Eli on how the game is played at this level. Kurt has a unique ability to read secondary coverages, get the ball out quickly in blitz situations, and create an up-tempo attack."

Warner and his new team surprised the NFL by winning five of their first seven games. But on November 14, after he had been sacked six times in a 17–14 loss at Arizona, the Giants' second in a row, Coughlin announced Manning would start the remaining games of the season.

Warner was extremely disappointed. He had launched an incredible comeback for himself, apparently to no avail. Nevertheless, he handled his situation to the admiration of all. In the locker room, during the quarterback meetings, on the practice field, from the sideline, he was the Giants'— and Manning's—loudest cheerleader.

"If Kurt wasn't handling this so graciously," said New York fullback Jim Finn, "this would be an even bigger mess."

Again, Warner said, he had focused on the Word. "What I saw during the period where football kind of got taken away from me was that I was probably more effective for God than I ever was when I was on top," Warner said. "Here's a chance to see, 'All those things he said when things were going well, is that really the way he lives his life?' What I've seen, what God showed me, is that exactly what happened in St. Louis over a seven-year period happened in one year. I truly think it's not a coincidence. I think God knew, 'I'm going to have him in New York for one year, so how can he be most effective for me?'"

In Warner's view, New York's 5–2 start served as a door opening to an NFL team where there wouldn't be a young star waiting for his turn. And for that, he was so very grateful. "All of it, I think, is done for a bigger purpose," he said. "Trying to keep my eyes fixed on that allowed me to handle it the way that I've handled it."

In 2005, with few NFL teams showing any interest in him—certainly not as a starter—Warner was signed for one year by the Arizona Cardinals. Head coach Dennis Green needed an experienced quarterback for a team hinting at a bright future, and Warner delivered. Warner was rewarded with a three-year $18 million contract that could be worth $20 million with incentives, and a few months later he was part of (what else?) another duel with a star rookie quarterback.

In April 2006, the Cardinals' No. 1 choice in the NFL draft was quarterback Matt Leinart, winner of the Heisman Trophy following a sensational career at the University of Southern California. In three years the 6'2", 225-pound Leinart

> "What I saw during the period where football kind of got taken away from me was that I was probably more effective for God than I ever was when I was on top."

had thrown for 10,693 yards (274 per game) and 99 touchdowns for the annually top-ranked Trojans.

Green chose Warner as the Cardinals' starting quarterback for 2006 but five weeks into the season replaced him with Leinart. Late in the year Leinart sustained a shoulder injury. Warner finished in fine fashion. In fact, anybody else likely would have settled in as the backup at such a stage of his career, but not Warner. Still convinced he could be an effective starter, he also had become extremely fond of throwing to the Cardinals' two fine young receivers, Larry Fitzgerald and Anquan Boldin.

"I don't want to be the cause of any other quarterback having to sit on the bench, but it drives me nuts not to be on the field leading my team," Warner said. "I honestly feel I can make a team better, that I can turn a game around."

New coach Ken Whisenhunt named Leinart his starter to open the 2007 season but after a few games replaced him with Warner, who responded with two compelling comeback victories. When Leinart went down with a broken collarbone at St. Louis in October, Warner took over and never looked back. "This is what you want to do every time you enter a season," he said. "Every time you come back to play, you want to be in there playing every snap. So I'm excited about that part of it. Obviously, I'm disappointed for Matt. You never want to get this position and take over a job due to an injury."

With 3,417 passing yards and 27 touchdowns—the team record is 28—Warner swept the Cardinals to an 8–8 record that suggested more victories were on the way. After the season was over, Whisenhunt named Leinart the starter for 2008.

It wasn't long, however, before he was emphasizing that Leinart would "be pushed" by Warner. That is precisely what transpired throughout a highly competitive training camp, after which Whisenhunt didn't announce the Cardinals' starting quarterback until the Saturday morning one week before the opening game at San Francisco.

> When Leinart went down with a broken collarbone at St. Louis in October, Warner took over and never looked back. "This is what you want to do every time you enter a season," he said. "Every time you come back to play, you want to be in there playing every snap."

In his first two NFL seasons, Leinart completed 56 percent of his passes for 3,134 yards and 13 touchdowns. He'd thrown 16 interceptions. In the same time, Warner completed 63 percent of his passes for 4,794 yards and 33 touchdowns. He'd thrown 22 interceptions.

"The person who best gives us a chance to win next Sunday at San Francisco is Kurt Warner," Whisenhunt said. "To the credit of both of our quarterbacks, it was close. It really came down to who I felt gave us the best chance to win that first game.

"It was a long decision. I was up most of the night and even this morning, going back over it, going through it. It's an important decision. We owed it to our ownership, our fans, and especially to our team."

Leinart's reaction was "what I'd hoped it would be," Whisenhunt said. "He's

upset. That's what you want to see. I saw the competitiveness in Matt come out. He is disappointed because he felt he'd made progress, and he has made progress. I'm very excited about the progress he's made and his future with this organization.

"No matter which way we went, somebody was going to be upset. I expected it."

Warner recalled his initial reaction to the news as bittersweet. "I was obviously excited for me and the opportunity, but I'm also disappointed for Matt," he said. "I know the position he's in and how difficult that is. But I'm definitely excited to have this opportunity. You have a quarterback of the future. Guys like me aren't going to be playing another 10 years. You're always looking for that next guy to run the show. Those guys get the benefit of the doubt."

Warner had in effect known similar challenges throughout his football career. At Northern Iowa. With the Amsterdam Admirals and Jeff Delhomme. The St. Louis Cardinals, with Tony Banks, Trent Green, and Mark Bulger. The New York Giants and Eli Manning.

He said that all he's ever asked for is the chance to compete, and Ken Whisenhunt had promised him that.

"It's very comforting. It says a lot about our staff and specifically Coach Whisenhunt. I thanked him. He's a man of his word. I really appreciate that," Warner said.

· 7 ·
PHILANTHROPY &
FAITH

Though the Warners have money now, Brenda insists that they know how to live with and without and that it's love that ultimately matters in their relationship.

Dishes clattered. The door on the microwave slammed. The dishwasher churned, the garbage was put out, a friend was at the front door, the TV droned in another room. Kids were screaming and crying.

Four kids: 13, 10, three, and a 16-month-old infant. Dad hammering another nail to straighten a picture frame; Mom cradling the baby with her bottle. Phone ringing again. Thump, thump, thumping from the stairwells. Bedrooms upstairs; meals on the main floor; air hockey, auto-racing machines, the pool table, and jukebox downstairs. Only as early evening approached did the perpetual motion and ambient clamor begin to relent around the dining room table where heads bowed, hands clasped, a prayer was spoken, dinner was served, and eventually the little ones went off to bed.

The home was on a knoll embraced by trees, a circular drive in front, sequestered behind walls, a gated residence of money. It had been only a few years since they had resided with little money in the chilly basement of her parents' home, she on food stamps, he working nights, their future together uncertain.

"Take all these things away, and we're still going to be the same," said Brenda. "When we were poor, we were just in love. We know how to live with and how to live without. Before, I couldn't afford bran cereal. Now he has a cereal named after him."

This was seven years ago, in the summer of 2002, when he was with the Rams and they lived in suburban St. Louis with their four children—before they moved to New Jersey in 2004 and a year later to Phoenix. They stayed in Arizona and now live in suburban Paradise Valley with their seven children (Zachary, 20; Jesse Jo, 18; Kade, 10; Jada Jo, 8; Elijah, 4, and twins Sienna and Sierra, 2).

It was in St. Louis that they were first exposed to national celebrity, when beyond the gates of their home everyone noticed them, occasionally stared at them, and sometimes even scrutinized them. "There are days I don't leave the gates," Brenda said then. "You can't 'recognize' us here."

But they never resented their notoriety. Instead they put it to work for themselves,

> "Take all these things away, and we're still going to be the same," said Brenda Warner. "When we were poor, we were just in love. We know how to live with and how to live without. Before, I couldn't afford bran cereal. Now he has a cereal named after him."

for their community, and ultimately for their God. The grand stage of the NFL provided a chance to lead and reach out to more people than either ever imagined. Initially, Kurt's stardom opened the doors to hospitals Brenda and he began to visit, for the bibles and CDs and children's games they gave away. "Before all this happened," Brenda said, "I doubt the hospitals would have let anyone come in and pray with these kids, just an open prayer like that, but they let us. So many of the children are just lying there full of radiation and tubes, and they're bald, they're pale, and they just light up when he walks in the room. Just light up!

"But it really does bless us more. When Zachary was injured, I told myself I'd never forget what it was like. The doctors said he wasn't going to live, knowing that they gave me no hope. All I wanted was someone to believe with me. Kurt was that someone. And now we're the ones to go in and be the people who give hope."

Mere months after the Rams defeated the Tennessee Titans 23–16 in the 2001 Super Bowl, Warner fulfilled a promise he had made to himself 15 years earlier as a boy growing up in Iowa. "I come from a lower income family and a background of volunteering and people giving back," he said. "There were some people who really made a difference in my life. I always had

Kurt and Brenda do work
for the Make-A-Wish
Foundation.

Life can be hectic around the Warner household. Their seven children keep Kurt and Brenda very busy.

the dream of playing in the NFL and I said that when I do, I'm going to give back. I finally made it with the Rams, and the foundation was something Brenda and I wanted to get going very quickly."

On May 1, 2001, the Warners launched the First Things First Foundation, and both were on the same page, chapter and verse: Matthew 6:33: "But seek first his kingdom and his righteousness, and all these things shall be yours as well."

There was so much to do, however, that they needed help. Warner asked the Rams' director of community relations, Marci Moran, if she might be available full-time.

"Quite honestly, my first answer was no," said Moran (now Pritts). "I had a great job with an NFL team. But then I got a two-page handwritten list of all the different programs and different things Kurt wanted to try to do with his foundation. He had put a lot of thought into it. He wasn't just doing it because 'I'm a big-name player now and I need a foundation.'"

Naming the foundation was easy. In January, minutes after his 73-yard touchdown pass to Isaac Bruce had defeated the Tennessee Titans in the Super Bowl, Mike Tirico of ABC-TV put the microphone to Warner before tens of millions on worldwide television: "Kurt! First things first, did you say anything before you guys went out for that play?"

"First things first, I gotta give the praise and glory to my lord and savior up above! Thank you Jesus!"

"It was the perfect lead-in," Warner says now. "When we decided to start the foundation, so many people remembered 'first things first.' Besides, it kind of encompassed my whole journey, where I had been, and what my life was really about."

Kurt and Brenda's First Things First Foundation includes a lot of phenomenal programs for children and families.

Warner obviously enjoys the "We're Going to Disney World" trip as much as the kids do!

The Warners' mission was to promote Christian values and—based upon their faith, family, and own experiences—to advance in life despite severe challenges and setbacks. Through their efforts and hands-on involvement, the foundation has expanded steadily over the last eight years while helping improve the lives of countless individuals and families in the United States and abroad.

Due in large measure to Brenda's training as a nurse, the Warners have a special connection with children who are battling illness and injuries. Among the many First Things First programs, several center around aid and support for children in hospitals in the St. Louis and Phoenix areas and in Iowa. The Basket of Hope program benefits newly diagnosed children and their families. Another program, Children's Hospital Outreach, includes Warner's Corner, which is a lounge established at Cardinal Glennon Children's Hospital, and NAME in Phoenix, where teens benefit from an environment created especially for them that includes sports memorabilia, large-screen TVs, computer games and more. More Warner's Corner areas in other health facilities are planned for the future.

Among the foundation's philanthropic activities is the collection of more than 90,000 winter coats in the St. Louis area during the Warners' Warm-Up Coat Drive and sponsoring weeklong trips for more than 30 Make-A-Wish families as part of the "We're Going to Disney World" annual event. The foundation has also provided game tickets to nearly 1,200 people and collected more than 15,000 pounds of gently used sports equipment for soldiers serving overseas as part of the foundation's second annual America's Team Ball Drive.

Kurt and Brenda enjoy nothing more than the good works they do for others in the name of their Christian values.

Warner on safari during the First Things First Foundation's "We're Going to Disney World" annual event.

After visiting flood-ravaged regions in 2008, including various areas in his home state of Iowa, Warner created a partnership with Habitat for Humanity to sponsor home builds throughout the Midwest that raised more than $650,000. "He is constantly asking, 'What else can I do?'" Moran said. "He is always looking for more opportunities. Everything he and Brenda do is somehow related to their lives. Special-needs kids, children in the hospital, it's all part of their background. We work with Homes for the Holidays to help low-income single parents become homeowners because Brenda was a low-income single mom struggling on food stamps, living in public housing."

"The Lord has given us a responsibility, whether it's the faith part of it or the financial part of it," Kurt says. "It goes way back to when Brenda and I first began dedicating our lives to the lord and not having very much. He could trust us with those little things, and he knows that by blessing us now with so much, we were going to take care of it and be good stewards to his word, to his kingdom."

"We want to branch out and influence people all over the country," Warner said. "To us it's not about, 'Okay, we live here, so let's affect this community.' How many people can we affect? What kind of difference can we make, expand in different cities, different areas? Wherever and however."

In May 2001, not long after they had started First Things First, Luke Maue, 7, came to Rams Park with his Boy Scout troop. Everyone got to meet Kurt Warner. Kurt Warner threw his arms around them, learned their names, and took them on a tour of the indoor practice field, the weight room, and the locker room. He treated every Scout as if he was his son, autographed their shirts and caps and footballs, then gave each of them a huge hug when it was time for them to go.

Two weeks later Luke Maue was on another Boy Scouts tour when he was run over and killed by a drunk driver outside the St. Louis Zoo.

Brenda went to the wake. His parents told her Kurt had been their son's hero and gave her Luke's favorite hat. Brenda took it home and handed it to her husband. He signed it, "Luke, say hi to Jesus for me. I'll see you there." The hat was buried with Luke in the coffin.

It was as Brenda drove away from the funeral that she thought of Luke's coffin and what it must have cost, because she remembered so vividly what had happened after her parents were killed by the tornadoes. A $1,500 invoice for their cremation had come in the mail, and she couldn't believe it. "I couldn't believe I had to write that check," she said.

She called the funeral home to find out if the $1,500 was for one or both of her parents. What a question to have to ask!

"Honey," the man told her gently on the phone, "the Red Cross took care of that for you."

"I never forgot that man's words, so respectful and assuring," Brenda said.

> "I think people want to see the real deal, they want to see someone who not only talks it but walks it, someone who's faced a lot of situations and continues to hold strong to [his] faith. And hopefully, through the mountaintops and valleys, I've stayed consistent with what I speak and what I believe. Because of that, I think people have nothing to attack."

"And I remember feeling blessed that I did not have to write that check. So when I'm driving home, I thought, those parents had to write the check for Luke's casket. Immediately I called Marci and said let's make sure that any child under 12 killed in the St. Louis area, we pay for the casket."

Among the first things Warner did after signing with the Giants in 2004 was call Moran, who recalled, "His first word to me was, 'Expand.'" There were to be no cutbacks on the foundation's contributions to any programs in the St. Louis area; instead, the new goal was to add as many programs as possible in the New York area.

"When we go and do these programs," Warner says, "when we spend time at Disney with the Make-A-Wish kids or we do the Special Olympics thing, we have more fun with it than the actual participants do. I'm not sure if that's fair or not. We're running it and we're having more fun. Everybody who has gotten involved with us, I think, has seen the same thing.

"It's been so rewarding for our children too. We want this to be a family foundation. Getting them involved and staying involved as a family has truly humbled us and kept us focused on the right things."

It keeps growing, largely because of Warner's effort, dedication and input.

"To me, all these doors are opening up," he says. "People say, 'He's leaving St. Louis, so I guess that door closed and all those things stop.' In my opinion, the doors just keep opening, and I want to keep them open. I want to be able to go back into St. Louis and do things there. I want to be able to go to Iowa, go to New York. If I ever play anywhere else, if I ever move anywhere else, I look at it like a bunch of doors opening because of the opportunities I've had."

"His heart is in the right place," says Marci Pritts. "He is obviously a Christian man. His faith is the root of everything he and his wife do in the community. It is not for the PR, it is not for marketing purposes. It is because they are doing what God calls them to do."

In December 2006, Warner was interviewed for the website of Busted Halo Ministries, an outreach of the Paulist Fathers, a religious order of Roman Catholic priests. The questions asked of him by Trish Muco-Tobin were fair and to the point, and Warner's answers were direct and unwavering.

Q: Do you feel your persona as a man of faith is met with skepticism by the public and the media?

A: I think people want to see the real deal, they want to see someone who not only talks it but walks it, someone who's faced a lot of situations and continues to hold strong to [his] faith. And hopefully, through the mountain-tops and valleys, I've stayed consistent with

> "I think God meets us all in different places and different times but I think the goal is to keep seeking him. He's not elusive, he's not trying to miss us, he's there for us...look for him in each and every circumstance because he's there, and he wants to be found."

what I speak and what I believe. Because of that, I think people have nothing to attack. They were probably skeptical at the beginning. When [the Rams] were having so much success, it was easy for all of us to say, "Thank You, Jesus," and then when things don't go so well, you never hear it again. But I think through the course of things, I've been consistent enough and unwavering in my faith—no matter the circumstances—and that's why people have accepted me for who I am. There are some people out there who preach the message that a strong faith equals worldly success. I don't buy into any of that.

Q: Do you believe success is related to the strength of one's faith?

A: Unfortunately, a lot of times faith and success go hand-in-hand. When somebody is successful, their faith level seems higher. There are some people who preach the message that a strong faith equals worldly success, but I don't buy into any of that. I was just reading a book that said something like, "You don't know that God is all you need until you're in a position where he's all you've got." To find out what somebody's truly about, where their faith really is, is when they struggle.

Q: Since leaving the Rams in 2003, it's been a difficult ride for you. What's it like to descend from such a high?

A: Any time you're considered the best at what you do for a period of time, it's hard to settle for anything less.... So when things didn't go my way, bouncing around from team to team, I had a perspective that God wanted to do something with me in every one of those situations. I never want to come to a realization that maybe what I accomplished in the NFL is all I'm supposed to accomplish.

Q: After having lived on both sides, how has your perspective changed about American celebrity and the public's obsession with it?

A: You have to be careful. With success comes great opportunities and also great temptation. The greater the platform, the more people are watching, the greater chance you have to impact, but also the greater chance you have to impact people negatively. That's one thing I've learned. When you grow up dreaming about playing football, you never think of what's outside the lines...you have to come to realize the responsibility that comes with it, and that's probably the biggest lesson I've learned about fame.

Q: Would you advise young adults to seek God in the same way?

A: Yes, if you're searching and seeking, and you're looking in the right places, you'll find him. I think God meets us all in different places and different times but I think the goal is to keep seeking him. He's not elusive, he's not trying to miss us, he's there for us...look for him in each and every circumstance because he's there, and he wants to be found.

In the weeks leading up to last February's Super Bowl, the Warners discussed at length whether the Cardinals game against the Steelers would be his last—win or lose. For as long as he'd been a quarterback in the pros, from Des

Kurt and Brenda credit God with bestowing so many blessings upon them, the largest of which is their beautiful children.

Warner has paid a heavy physical price for all he has achieved and has considered retirement in recent years.

Moines to Amsterdam to St. Louis to New York to Phoenix, there had been so many days, weeks, and months when he had been hurting. If it wasn't bad ribs, a broken finger, or a sprained thumb, it was a concussion, pulled groin, or vocal chords so bruised he could not speak.

As recently as last March—days after signing a two-year contract with the Cardinals for $23 million—it was hip surgery. By all accounts he will be fit to lead the team he needs—and that needs him—this fall. None of it matters to the kids, though. He's Dad, and when he walks through the door they want a piece of him, a major piece of him.

"We have all these blessings God has given us," Brenda was saying in the summer of 2002. "We teach our kids about them, and then I see Kurtis pay the price. He's hurting, and the kids still want him to play. They want to roll on the floor with him, they want to wrestle. He's like, 'It's okay,' and he gets out of the aching, bent-over, and bruised kind of feeling and goes on and is just Dad. I've seen him wince in pain. And when we're in bed and he can't even move, I know how much pain he's in. I'm a nurse and can't help."

> "We have all these blessings God has given us," Brenda was saying in the summer of 2002. "We teach our kids about them, and then I see Kurtis pay the price. He's hurting, and the kids still want him to play. They want to roll on the floor with him, they want to wrestle. He's like, 'It's okay,' and he gets out of the aching, bent-over, and bruised kind of feeling and goes on and is just Dad."

Marshall Faulk, his All-Pro backfield partner in St. Louis, remembers. "We were a bunch of losers, pretty much," he says of the team Warner emerged to command in 1999.

"The Rams had lost, the coach had lost, we had all had our butts kicked. It wasn't like we were this powerhouse that just plugged a new quarterback in and continued to roll. We were bad. We were all saying, 'Who's this 13?' I think he threw three touchdowns in each of the first three games, and I thought, *Okay, I'll wait. We haven't hit a real bumpy road yet.* Then we played Tennessee, we're 6–0 and we're down 21–6, and they were just teeing off on Kurt. And I always felt like when a quarterback is getting smacked around, you really get to see who this guy is. And he'd come back to the huddle, and he wouldn't ask for more time, he wouldn't ask the guys to hold their blocks, he would just call the play, drop back, throw the ball, get hit. After the game, it was brutal. He got beat up. He never said a word, never bitched, never screamed.

"From that point forward, I knew this guy was special."

Warner admits that initially the
public may have been skeptical of his
benevolence, but he feels that time,
consistency, and God have helped prove
the selflessness of his good works.